Perry Wood

Secrets
of the
People
Whisperer

A Horse Whisperer's Techniques
for Enhancing Communication
and Building Relationships

MJF BOOKS
NEW YORK

Published by MJF Books
Fine Communications
322 Eighth Avenue
New York, NY 10001

Secrets of the People Whisperer
LC Control Number 2006940503
ISBN-13: 978-1-56731-870-8
ISBN-10: 1-56731-870-3

QM   10 9   8   7   6   5   4   3   2   1

Dedicated to my dear Esaya;
you gave me so much:
I had never experienced such freedom and joy
until you came into my life
and shared those gifts with me.
God bless your soul

Table of Contents

Acknowledgements

Heartfelt thanks to my family, friends and all those who have given me their support.

My thanks and respect to Judith Kendra at Rider for her vision, gentleness and professionalism in publishing this book, and to all at Random House who have contributed in bringing this book to life and out into the world.

Thanks to all at Ulysses Press for their input and guidance.

Thanks and unconditional love to Tenor for being a loyal companion.

Love and thanks to Monte (and his band of happy followers) for setting a great example in how to be a kind, noble and powerful leader.

Thanks to Andrew McFarlane, Elaine Harrison and all at Leadchange: I could not have wished for better people to work with and have as partners. Thanks also to Andrew for being such a model of integrity, and to Elaine for speaking with such intuitive insight that I have, on occasions, been literally floored; she has given and continues to give so much as a partner, friend, guide and Goddess!

Love and thanks to Margrit Coates for being my guardian angel.

Thanks to all of my coaching clients and students: coaching and learning are two-way streets, which mean you have helped and taught me at least as much as I have taught you.

Thanks to Kate Parkes for offering such gems of wisdom just when I need them.

Huge thanks to all the people whom I have found challenging, difficult, scary or downright impossible over the years: you may have contributed more to my writing this book than anyone else!

My appreciation to "the family" at Mataji Yogananda's center in Somerset for your work in bringing the gifts of pure meditation and Kriya Yoga to so many people, including myself: it really is priceless, thank you.

Finally, thanks to anyone who reads this book and, as a result of using the secrets of the people whisperer in their lives, makes the world a more joyful place for themselves and others to live in.

Perry Wood
August 2005

Introduction

I am in the car with my father. We are on our way to the coast to spend a couple of days together. I have a sense that he is seriously ill and may not last beyond Christmas: it is now the end of October. I am afraid about this, not because we are very close, but because we are not very close. We have not really communicated, except on a superficial level, for years.

I had asked him to come away with me so that we might talk. I wanted to make my peace with him; there were things I felt I needed to know from him before he was gone forever and time was running out. Normally it was my mother who did most of the talking while my father lived almost silently in his own reclusive world: reading a novel, watching TV or listening to music with his headphones on.

For the first couple of hours on the journey I was asking myself whether this was such a good idea. Our conversation was on the usual superficial level and I wondered if we were going to get on to anything meaningful that I wanted to hear from him.

Suddenly the conversation opened up: he began to talk and didn't stop talking for two whole days. He told me stuff I wanted to know, stuff I'd wondered about and stuff that had never even entered my head. He told me the reasons why he hadn't wanted children and the reasons he'd decided to have them anyway. He told me how it was for him as a child and how it was for him when he had small children of his own. He told me how money had been for him. He told me how much he loved my mother. He told me how much he loved my brother and me and how proud he was of us. He talked about sex. He told me what he was afraid of, what his fears were and what hurt him even after many decades had passed. He told me things that I hold in my heart and cannot share with you or anyone else.

By releasing all the things that he had kept locked up for so long, by communicating openly and honestly, I finally understood so much about him, and about myself, too. By what he communicated, he had freed me, and I hope that in some way he had freed himself.

Following the trip away with my father, I began to think about all of the significant relationships in my life, past and present, and the effects that communication had on them. I reflected on what adults had communicated to us as children, about how my parents had communicated with each other, how I had lost close touch with my brother. I reflected on how, despite there being a great deal of love, so much of my marriage had been nine years of anger, frustration, feeling unloved, lonely and misunderstood, and how this had finally led to divorce. How the business I had co-run for twelve years, although successful, had been an uphill struggle because of how my partner and I communicated with each other, our staff, suppliers and clients.

It seemed that I had been brilliant at saying the wrong thing, at hurting people's deepest feelings, at being misunderstood or misinterpreting what someone was telling me without ever intending to do so.

If my mouth was open, I would put my foot in it. If there was something teeth-jarringly inappropriate to say, I would say it. If there was a way to appear completely uncaring, I would find it.

The two days with my father were a crystallization of a mystery, the answers to which I had been searching for for fifteen years. What I searched for and began to discover are the "secrets of the people whisperer." Though I should really say re-discovered, for although some of the methods presented in this book may appear to be totally new, they have always been there, despite remaining largely hidden from many of us.

Communication, whether good or bad, is a huge issue in every area of all of our lives: in our intimate relationships, personal, business, family and friendships. How wonderful and liberating would it be then, to become a highly skilled communicator? A people whisperer? What would it be like to truly understand other people and to be truly understood, to move effortlessly through life with more ease, love, fun and joy?

Everything that happens communicates something. Everything we think, do or say is a communication—which means it gives out a message—and each and every message has an impact on shaping our lives, for better or for worse: even love itself is a form of communication. This raises all kinds of exciting possibilities and questions . . .

✦ How do you communicate with your partner or loved ones?
✦ What are you communicating to your environment?
✦ What kind of communications happen in your workplace or business?
✦ If you have a spiritual guide or God in your life, how do you communicate with them and how do you hear what they communicate to you?
✦ Most fundamentally: how do you communicate with yourself?

The answers to these questions are some of the secrets of people whispering; that means to be aware of what you and other people are communicating on every level, mentally, verbally, physically and spiritually, and to be adept at interacting with kindness, under-standing, skill, power and subtlety.

The secrets of people whispering work in every situation in our lives: from intimate relationships with loved ones to work environments, even to situations where we and our enemies meet. Some people have always had a few pieces of the jigsaw, some part of the secrets, but it is only now, in the twenty-first century, the "Communication Age," with cell phones, text messaging, e-mails, the Internet and all manner of communication mediums, that the secrets of people whispering have been drawn together in such a way.

I have been very fortunate in needing to improve my communication skills so badly. I was "asking" to learn and, as the saying goes, "When the pupil is ready, the teacher appears." And my teachers did appear.

My master teachers communicate at a very subtle level. They have refined their skills over the last sixty million years to a very high degree and their very survival depends upon it. They do not use words and do not judge; they are noble, quick-witted and very powerful; they sense true intentions, integrity and have an innate sense of justice. These master teachers are horses. When you get your communication wrong with a person, you may end up having an argument or someone sulking. When you get it wrong with half a ton of hyper-sensitive flight animal, you know about it!

I spent a number of years studying some of the great riding masters. I worked training, breeding and starting (breaking in) young horses and developing ways to communicate with these magnificent creatures. My experiences ultimately led to me writing a groundbreaking book about my approach with horses, in order to share some of the knowledge I had accumulated.

As my life and experience with horses expanded, I spent a great deal of time working at the occluded front where horses and people meet: teaching people to improve their communication with horses and, as an unintended side effect, helping people to discover how they communicate with themselves and with each other.

My experiences of horse whispering led me to see horses as a mirror: they reflect back very clearly whatever it is that you are communicating to them. I then realized that people do the same thing: they also reflect your communications back to you, although it can be difficult to see this because the use of words, judgments, gossip, social masks and preconceived notions often act as a smoke screen.

The discoveries about communication that were surfacing as a result of my years as a professional horseman took me on to another unintended path. I found myself delivering "breakthrough" workshops with horses, coaching couples on their relationship issues and executives from international corporations in their leadership and communication skills. My work had taken me from horse whispering into people whispering, so to speak. Both require a high degree of self- and other-awareness, so that you know exactly what you are communicating, even if it is unintentional, and to truly listen to what others are communicating.

During my work coaching executives in corporations, as well as couples and individuals, I have seen more and more how we shape every aspect of our lives by the way we communicate with ourselves and others. These communications are often so automatic or so subtle that we are oblivious to them and really do not know what we are communicating: the secrets of people whispering will bring light into your relationships and give you the means to create immediate and profound improvements to every interaction you have.

Secrets of the People Whisperer will show you simple and incredible ways to connect with your true self, other people and the world at large on many different levels. It will show you how to understand and be understood; to truly listen and give people space in which they can express themselves without fear or judgment. It will also enable you to ask for what you want from the universe itself and have a far greater chance of getting it. (What is meant by "universe" in the context of this book is anything and everything other than your body and your conscious thoughts: you may wish to think of it as your higher self, your subconscious, the environment, God or whatever else makes sense to you.) Through its guidance, you will come to know others and yourself better on physical, mental and energy levels; you will begin to go beyond personality and allow the true "being" within yourself and other people to shine through. Ultimately, you will discover how to give every relationship and meeting you ever have the best possible chance of success.

In order to gain the most from this book, I would suggest that you read one chapter at a time so that you absorb the essence of each secret before moving on to the next one.

When you make use of the *Secrets of the People Whisperer* in your life—at home, at work and at play—it is not a gift from me to you, it is a gift from you to yourself and to your loved ones. Out of love and respect for yourself and the people in your life, I urge you to give and receive that gift and enjoy the kind of experiences you deserve.

My sense about my father's illness around Christmastime had been right. On Boxing Day he suddenly became very ill, doubled up with pain in his stomach. He was rushed to hospital where it was discovered that he was suffering from previously undiagnosed cancer in his gut, and worse, the cancer had punctured a hole through the lining of the gut and caused peritonitis. He was operated on immediately and miraculously survived. Afterward, the surgeon said that had they not operated on him that day he would have been dead the next.

PART I

Whispering to Yourself

SECRET ONE
Be Who You Really Are

Who Are You Really?

You don't have to know anything about horses to understand what I am about to tell you. You may equally have spent years around horses and formed a totally different opinion from the one below. But please read on, with an open mind, because what I have written below is completely true for me and—in being true—it will more than likely match with something of your own life experience. For what I say about horses also seems to be true about people, too . . .

During my many years spent working closely with horses, I have come to realize something wonderful and daunting: horses are always totally 100 percent themselves. And because horses are always totally 100 percent themselves, like fully enlightened people, they can see when we are not being our true selves. This presents us with a great gift, and sometimes a great challenge. You could say that horses don't respond to how we think we are, but how we really are; and that they don't respond to what we think we are saying, but what we are really saying.

Around horses I have pretended to be brave and courageous, angry, loving, a leader, empathic, strong, determined, confident, quiet, soft and gentle, and many other things, but because I was pretending, the horses knew I wasn't being true. There have been times with horses when I have acted calmly when in fact I have been scared witless; there have been times when I have acted happy when I was seething with anger at the horse's behavior; and there have been times when I have endeavored to show my light side, when in fact my darker, shadow side has been ruling me. Although the horses made some gestures of recognition for how I was pretending to be, what they really saw and responded to was my true inner state.

It is possible to stroke or pat a horse with your hand; it is also possible to do it with your heart. It is possible to act like a horse's leader; it is also possible to *be* a leader. It is possible to appear to be bold and courageous, caring or loving; it is also possible to *be* all of those things. The truth is that horses always know the difference between what you appear to be and who you really are. By using body language, mental communication and creating soul connections, the horses around me seem to reflect, like four-legged, living, breathing, sentient mirrors, more and more about who I really am. Because they mirror things back so clearly, it means I am required to acknowledge truths about myself, including truths that I desperately pretend aren't there, truths I haven't wanted others to see and truths I even hide from myself.

Traits such as a shortage of patience, lack of confidence, insincerity, over-ambition, fears, anger etc. have all surfaced in one way or another with horses. It is not all bad: as these things are brought to light they are given the chance to be recognized, acknowledged and perhaps healed. And what is more, by acknowledging the truths about ourselves, we also begin to see our positive qualities, our light, brilliance, magnificence, depth, love, tenderness and infinite essence. Strangely, it is often the case in our society that it is easier for us to acknowledge our "negative" qualities than it is our "positive" ones.

Despite the challenges brought about by acknowledging who we really are, warts and all, there also comes a huge sense of relief, joy and bliss. It takes so much energy and effort to be who we are not, and yet it is so normal for us to do that, so by the time we have past early childhood, it seems to us that it is normal. Mad, but normal! Thank God, then, that creatures such as horses can bring us back to being who we really are.

Of course you can be effective around horses and never go beyond the surface layers. You can make horses be your servants, force them to win competitions, make them run until they drop, say they are stupid or lack intellect as we know it, but you may miss one of the greatest opportunities to free yourself that life has to offer: an opportunity to be who you really are.

Being with horses is not the only way to become who we really are. People can also help us to make these discoveries, although the ways in which people mirror us are often more complex or disguised. Ultimately, everything and everyone in our lives can be seen as a reflection of who we really are: loving, playful, enquiring, crazy beings in a universe of endless wonders.

People whisperers are aware that human beings exist on many different levels—physical, mental, emotional and spiritual—and they interact with other people on all of these levels in their relationships and communications. To do this requires people whisperers to be who they really are.

During every single relationship or communication you ever have there is always one regular participant: you. No matter how much time you spend with your partner, loved ones, family, friends or work colleagues, there is one person you will always spend more time with than with any of them: you. It isn't very easy to know anyone *really* well and the person who is often the hardest to *really* know is yourself.

So the first question is: **how do you find out who you really are?**

Let's ask another question: who are you not? You're *not* any one of the other six billion or so humans on the planet . . . That means you are totally unique. Wow! Let's think about that for a moment: there is no one else among an unimaginable six billion people who has your fingerprints, your eyes, your teeth, your body, your personality, your experiences or your thoughts. That means you're absolutely incredible. In the vastness of time and space, from the Big Bang onward into the eternal future, across the infinity of the universe, no one will ever be you—except you. That's big! It makes you special beyond words.

Who else are you *not*? You're not the habits, behaviors, characteristics or beliefs that you have learned or picked up from other people. Anything you do to *try* to get someone's approval is not you either! You are *you*—a unique, perfect and powerful being and when you stop trying to do anything because you think you "should" you are incredible.

So what would you like to do with your unique and extraordinary life? Will you create love or hate, beauty or a mess? What would you like to express? Who would you like to touch in some way? What difference do you really want to make?

It is important to realize that however small your life may seem to you, the universe will know. It will notice what you have done, are doing and will do while you're here in this life. Your presence is making a difference: it is impossible for it to do otherwise.

So who are you exactly? Are you your body? Are you your mind? Did you first come into being when you were born? Did you exist in any form before you were conceived? Part of you is your body and part of you is your mind: but what if your body is just a suit that you are wearing until it wears out, or a costume you are wearing for a role in a play, and when the performance is over you'll take it off again? What if your mind, "personality" or self-identity is a role you are playing in some kind of cosmic theatrical production? And when this performance is over you will stop pretending to be the "person" you think you are and go back to being your real self instead . . .

What if your mind is a computer that was completely empty when you were born, but other people have been filling it with "stuff" since then, so it's now so clogged up with spam, old programs and deleted files you don't know which bits you need and which bits you don't. And sometimes it crashes for no reason whatsoever!

In truth, our bodies are amazing machines and much of what is programmed into our minds is fabulously useful, but if our bodies are temporary suits and our minds are sometimes rebellious computers, what else is there that makes us who we really are? What other parts of you are there when your body is still and your thoughts stop? Your body has probably changed through the time you've had it (I know mine has!), and your mind is constantly developing and being fed new information, so what is there about you that is a constant? Somewhere inside, do you feel like the same person now as you always were: the same now as when you were a small child even? When you communicate with yourself, do you sometimes have a sense of that unchanging person inside?

In case you are asking yourself what all this has to do with people whispering, the answer is that when you are being who you really are, everything flows, including your communication. When you are being who you really are, people can have a relationship with the real you, rather than a mask, an actor, a persona or phantom. And as we will see in later chapters, much of our communication occurs on a very subtle level, beyond the body and mind.

"THE REAL YOU" BEYOND BODY AND MIND

Many people talk about the soul, spirit, higher self, essence or other terms for that part of you that isn't your body and mind. Some people deny its existence because—they argue—we can't see it, measure it or prove it is there. To define the soul in words, ideas or thoughts seems practically impossible, but that is because it is beyond the body and mind.

We all know what the phrase "put soul into it" means; when you put soul into something it has a power that really touches people.

Put soul, love and your real self into your communications with others and see what incredible things start to happen.

POWERFUL PEOPLE WHISPERERS

Have you noticed how some people really inspire you, not by what they say or do or what their bodies look like (although that can be very interesting!) but just by being totally themselves? When you meet someone who is being who they really are, it touches something deep within you: their soul touches your soul. They touch something in you that yearns to be touched—to be let out into the light, to be recognized, to be freed to work the miracles that your own resources of love can perform for you.

In a relationship or communication where one person is being who they really are, it gives those around them the chance to be who they really are too: this is the magic of people whispering and real loving connection in action.

When I work with people and they have even a momentary glimpse into the cavernous infinity of their true inner self, they are stunned, elated and awestruck by the realization of their true potential. Yet each and every one of us has this vastness and potential within us: in truth, everyone is a powerful People Whisperer.

Things to do:
1. Look at your hand for a minute or two. Move the fingers around, pick things up, scratch your nose—be amazed! Advancements in science haven't come anywhere near to doing what you can do so effortlessly with just one hand! Watch yourself performing complex tasks like driving a car or making coffee totally automatically.

2. It is said that the eyes are the "windows of the soul." Go really close to the mirror with your face and look deeply into the pupils of your own eyes. How does it make you feel? Awestruck, afraid, uncomfortable, embarrassed, filled with love, uplifted, nothing whatsoever? Stay there for a while and feel whatever comes up. Do you notice yourself looking at one eye more than the other? Do you feel you have to keep looking away? Do you feel drawn further in?

   What is it like if you look deeply into your own eyes when you are upset with someone or something?

   What is it like if you look deeply into the eyes of another person (with their permission)? Take a non-judgmental and unhurried look into their soul by looking deeply into the pupils of their eyes.

3. Go somewhere busy where there are lots of people and take some time to watch them all. Marvel at how much variety there is: see how no one looks just like you; notice how each person has his or her own unique presence.

4. Place your attention inside yourself and get in touch with the unchanging, inner "you" that has been the same since your earliest memories.

5. Check out your body—what it looks like and what you feel about it. Think about all the things you might use your body for during the course of a normal week: walking, eating, sitting, expressing, opening doors, lifting things, laughing, having sex, writing, blowing your nose, eating, drinking, playing, hugging, smelling, touching, feeling pain, talking and hearing.

6. Marvel at how useful and brilliant your mind is: see how it can plan ahead, remember details, operate your body, analyze situations, sort out problems, create problems (oh dear!), make decisions, engage in conversations and many more things too numerous to mention.

Judgment

One of the major ways we can sabotage our relationships and not be who we really are is by being judgmental. We can spend so much time judging ourselves and the people around us that it becomes normal and we don't even notice we're doing it. We judge our behavior, our performance, our looks, our experiences, our responses and abilities in everything we do, and we judge other people in the same ways.

Being judgmental is a social addiction. Read the papers and you will see judgment, judgment, and judgment. Listen to people speak about themselves or others: judgment again. Act like a fly on the wall in practically every home, workplace or drinking bar in the world and you will overhear conversation that is carrying judgment with it.

Judgment creates a vicious circle: if every time you do something you are judged for it, you become less willing to take action, take risks, be creative or be yourself because you think you will be judged again—which you will be, by yourself if not by others! By constantly going over mistakes and shortcomings—real or imagined—you can become stuck in a life of limitation, which means you stop being who we really are, in the hope of avoiding being judged.

> Highly successful people don't hang around judging or beating themselves up for failures; they just get on with it.

JUDGING OTHER PEOPLE

In reality, you don't even have to express a judgment of someone verbally for that person to sense it: they unconsciously feel you judging them. When you judge someone, even if they are a thousand miles away, that judgment will somehow find its way to causing harm. If you always spoke about other people as though they were standing right next to you, how might you change what you say about them?

LETTING GO OF JUDGMENT

You can let go of judgment by accepting yourself, other people and situations just the way they are, not good or bad, just simply as they are. It can take a huge leap of consciousness to do that, because we are trained and imbued with a judgmental way of viewing the world from our earliest years. Of course things may not be ideal and you may wish to set about changing them, which is fine, but done without judging it "good" or "bad" will bring more clarity to your action.

When you don't judge people they are inexplicably drawn to you; they enjoy spending time with you because there is a freedom in your company that is rarely felt or seen. This is one of the most powerful, passive and wonderful ways to be a people whisperer: drop judgment. Simple!

When you communicate with another person and don't judge them, you become a light of attraction, because you allow them the freedom to express themselves and be who they really are: you create a "safe space" for them.

Things to do:

1. Where are you right now reading this book? Are there any people around? If so, take a look at them now (if not, think about people you know). What do you think of them? What do you think they are like? How do you know that's true? What effect does your thinking have on your behavior toward them? Can you look at them with total clarity: completely without judgment?

2. Start to notice how you judge yourself verbally or internally. This can be quite difficult to do at first because it is so habitual

that we just don't realize. Pick some obvious examples such as when you say you are "good" or "bad" at something. Start to notice what self-judgments come out of your mouth: listen to the words you speak and how you use them to limit yourself.

3. Observe how you label and judge things. Watch other people doing this habitually and see how it gets in the way of their relationships.

4. Experiment with being around people and not judging them at all, even in your mind. You may find yourself going a little quiet—that's because once we drop judgment, even on a subtle level, much of what we normally say becomes irrelevant.

Risking Being Open

To be who you really are requires you to risk being open; that means being open to the incredible things that life has to offer, such as joy, love, beauty, success, play, laughter, but also being open to hurt, struggle, grief or loss . . . it seems you can't have one without the other.

To experience life fully means being open to whatever other people bring into your life too: generally speaking, the most fun you can have, and some of the worst times you can have, are all to do with the people in your life.

Being open is a two-way street: open to receive and also open to give. You can be open to understanding someone else's feelings and open to sharing your own feelings. You can be open to accepting someone else's reality and open to sharing your reality honestly with someone else. You can be open to new experiences and be open to showing new experiences to someone else.

Being open to who we really are inevitably means risking the unknown. Without going into the unknown all we would ever do is go around in the same circle, treading the same groove and being stuck in a rut.

It is often only by taking the risk of losing that we can gain and move forward. It is really only the ego that fears being hurt: the real you, "who you really are" is impervious to pain.

It is impossible for life to stand still; it would probably be easier for us to walk on water than to make life stand still, but a fear of being open to the new often makes us try to do just that.

Being open means stepping outside your regular comfort zone, lowering your defenses, or dropping your familiar secure routines. And being open means being totally honest with yourself about what you are like and what you are experiencing.

> *Being open means ceasing to pretend to be someone you are not: what a relief to know that it is OK to think what you want to think and be honest about how you really feel, without wondering if it is "acceptable" to think or feel that way.*

Things to do:

1. Think of areas in which you are afraid to be open, such as your relationships at home or at your work. Now look at other people you know of who are going unharmed into the same areas in their lives as the ones you are afraid of: what is it that they do, say, believe etc. that is different to you and enables them to be open and safe?

2. Think about some of your more intimate moments: does anything hold you back? What would you say or do if you dared to? Think how you could allow yourself to express your love more freely.

3. Trust that you will be OK, that the real you cannot be harmed, regardless of how difficult things may be on the surface. Think about a time in your life when things were difficult or dangerous and acknowledge that you survived to live another day.

You could say that being *who you really are* is the single most important step in becoming a people whisperer, because by being who you really are, your communications and relationships all become "real," open and honest.

When you drop any form of judgment and simply accept others and yourself as you really are, more connectedness comes into your life, which means all of your communications and relationships are transformed: with yourself, other people and the universe.

SECRET TWO
Listen to Yourself

I am riding a horse that is refusing to move forward; he only wants to turn around and run for home. This behavior is becoming serious, because in order to get his own way, he has started rearing up, a potentially dangerous maneuver for him and me. The more unsure and fearful my thoughts and emotions become, the more the horse pushes the boundaries of what is safe by rearing higher and higher. It is as though he can hear me thinking about my own physical safety and detects my weakening resolve. Then something changes in me: by force of will I drop the disempowering thoughts about my safety and begin thinking that "maybe today is a good day to die; if we both crash to the ground and die together today that is OK."

This is not a sham: at that moment I am prepared to die. The horse senses this change and reflects that he doesn't want to kill us both today. He thinks about his actions and quits rearing. He puts all four feet back on the ground and moves forward. I let him know what a great horse he is and thank God I am still alive.

Horses naturally spend a large portion of their time in a state of fear. This is because horses are prey animals and are instinctively programmed to be alert and on the lookout for danger from predators. Despite humans being predators, in this day and age, it seems humans live in a state of fear much of the time too.

Until I spent my life with horses, I had not realized how much I lived in a state of fear or how much my fearful thoughts, emotions and projections impacted on what was actually happening around me. Because horses are so finely tuned to subtle signals, changes of energy, emotions and body language, they often appear to have ESP (extra sensory perception). When I realized horses were like this I thought it was very exciting, but then I started to understand it meant I had to become totally aware of what I was thinking or feeling. And the fact is horses *do* pick up on what we think and feel. Channeled in positive ways this can create incredible moments between man and beast, but when our thoughts or emotions are negative, e.g. fearful, the horses pick that up too.

In my early years with horses I had a very "jumpy" mare that would spook and be afraid of everything from a small bird in the hedge to a patch of different colored grass on the ground. To her it was a habit and a game, but basically she lived on fear and epinephrine. It didn't take long for her to affect me so that when I was riding her I felt the same fear she did. It got so bad I would need the bathroom five times before riding her out because I was thinking of what might happen. This state became such a habit I had fearful thoughts on every other horse I rode and then they would start spooking, sensing my fear and acting out that fear.

I realized the "problem" was coming from me; I was creating it with my mind and emotions. I also realized the fear blocked our communication, so while we both panicked about imaginary dangers, we lost our sense of partnership and didn't communicate anything constructive to one another.

Before becoming aware of my thoughts and how the fear was created by me, it was as though I were powerless to do anything about it; the fears would run away with me, almost as though the horse was doing it "to me." With the awareness of where the fear was coming from, i.e. from my thoughts, I was gradually able to put my mind to more useful and constructive uses, such as focusing on relaxing my body or communicating more precise instructions to the horses about how they use their bodies. By giving the horses more positive physical directions, it affected their minds and emotions in a positive way too. Later, when I came to communicating or whispering with unbroken horses I intended to ride, it was essential to have made these realizations and to listen to my thoughts and emotions in order to influence the way the horses behaved.

I still have the original mare. She is now quite old but she still enjoys a quick leap away from a sparrow or blackbird; these days I usually laugh with her and at her little jokes.

EAVESDROPPING ON YOUR THOUGHTS

People whisperers listen attentively to their own thoughts and emotions; they know that their thoughts and emotions go out into the world as speech and action, influencing their own behavior and affecting the people around them.

Even if you chat away all day to other people, the first communication you have in any given situation is with yourself—in the form of your thoughts. The thoughts you have create your actions and are reflected in how you communicate with others. Thoughts can be incredibly powerful, wonderful and useful; they can also be very limiting, harmful and destructive. This is why one of the first steps toward successful people whispering is to explore your internal "talking," i.e. what you are thinking.

> In every situation, the first communication you have is with yourself: and the way you communicate with yourself determines all of your actions.

Because most of your thoughts aren't expressed verbally, it is easy to think that they don't really exist and just happen in some totally secret place inside your brain, but this is not the case. Even on a purely scientific level, thoughts actually exist as little electrochemical impulses.

It is impossible to have a thought without it being communicated
or reflected in some way; even our bodies "betray" us
by broadcasting our thoughts out into the universe
through subtle body language messages.

If our every thought is communicated outwardly in some way, perhaps now would be a good time to check out what we are thinking . . . Wow, that's a bit scary: what if the universe hears some of the rude, crude, hateful, jealous, deceitful, angry, greedy, naughty things we think? Don't worry, we're all doing it, and anyway, most of us don't truly wish harm to anyone, even to ourselves! (Of course, as we become more aware that our thoughts are being broadcast across the universe we may choose to think them with more care.)

✦ How would you describe the majority of your own thoughts? Accepting or judgmental? Helpful or unhelpful? Confidence-boosting or limiting? Inspiring or energy-draining? Loving or hateful? Enabling or restricting?

✦ What effect do you think your thoughts have on your communications with other people? What effect do they have, for example, on your loved ones, your colleagues and even your environment?

✦ Have you inherited your way of thinking about love, work, money, life or fun from anyone? If so, who? Has that way of thinking been helpful or harmful in the long run?

✦ What thoughts would you choose to broadcast to the universe? What might your thoughts be telling, or asking, the universe right now?

When you eavesdrop on your thoughts, which of the two columns below would they mostly fall into?

I just can't lose weight.	I just might buy a chocolate factory.
I'm useless at that.	I'll give it a shot.

Work is such a drag.	Work is great: I get a break from the kids.
I am always too tired to enjoy myself.	I'm going out again!
He makes me feel really useless.	He has a need to prove himself.
Where can I find the money from?	Money always finds me when I need it.
She is so pushy and rude.	Oh dear, she is very insecure.
Oh, my butt looks big in this.	I am a living Renoir painting!
I wish I was good at something.	I'm about to discover my real talents.
Every time I try that, it's a disaster.	I've learned quite a lot from results.
I never meet the right kind of people.	I'm highly selective about friends.
Business deals always fail on me.	I'm an adventurous entrepreneur; would you like to invest in this brilliant new idea I have for a world-beating company?

Eavesdropping on your thoughts is a powerful and effective tool for people whispering: it does not require you to change what you are thinking or tell you what you should be thinking. Just by listening to your thoughts as you have them, you become aware of how you are communicating with yourself and how those thoughts might shape your life. Once you listen to yourself and become aware of your thoughts, they tend to lose much of the influence they have over you.

JANET'S STORY

Janet is a very good doctor in a busy and demanding general practice surgery, but she didn't realize just how much her self-talk—the things she said to and thought about herself—made her life more difficult than it needed to be. So much of her conversation was filled with self-judgment about how she "should" do this or "should" do that, or how she wasn't very good at this or that.

Although she is a very attractive, intelligent and caring woman of thirty-five, she had never been in a serious relationship. She often talked about her longing for a meaningful relationship, but at the same time she said she'd probably never meet the man of her dreams. And, even if she did, she said he probably wouldn't be interested in her anyway. Her logic went that as no one suitable had wanted her so far, why should anyone want her now or in the future?

Janet had quite a few hobbies, all of which she excelled at, which was great—except that it gave her even less time in her already busy schedule to stop and relax. She played the flute in amateur music groups, painted in watercolors, worked out at the gym and loved rowing. But she was even tough on herself about her hobbies: rather than enjoying what she did as pastimes, she had high expectations of doing her hobbies as well as a professional might do them.

At one of our coaching sessions I said to her that it must be really hard to live her life as Janet; that, going by the things she thought and said, she really didn't make it easy for herself to have a nice time and that she put a lot of pressure on herself. I didn't think more about this comment until she came back from a much-needed walking vacation in France and said, "While I was away I was thinking about what you said and you're right: it is not easy being me and living my life, I am hard on myself."

It had taken a week of slowing down and having the space to step back from her routine life for Janet to be able to listen to herself and realize how she made her life so difficult. She looked quite different as a result of this revelation and became much more aware of how she had judged and pushed herself. She even stopped saying "I should" all the time, although it occasionally slipped out! Her newfound ability to listen to herself has enabled her to start making some liberating and exciting decisions about the kind of life she wants to create for herself and is accompanied by a new sense of lightness.

Things to do:

1. Make the time to listen to yourself—the things you think and say—as often as possible. You don't need to judge, change, justify, analyze or respond—just listen with objective interest to your own inner chatter. At first do this in quiet moments; with practice you will be able to do it in challenging situations such as during a heated or emotional exchange with someone else. Watch what happens.

2. See if you can trace the origin of some of your thoughts. Who was it that first introduced a particular idea or way of thinking to you? Write down or acknowledge in your mind who the originator of the thought might have been. See how you are freed from unhelpful thoughts once you know they're not the real "you."

3. Begin to notice other people's limiting thought patterns through the things they say (but resist the temptation to point out their self-limiting patterns to them unless they ask you). In what ways do you do the same thing?

4. Notice the sort of constructive thought patterns that successful, joyful and loving people have through the positive things they say. How might it help you to copy them in some ways?

5. Take note of how life or the universe seems to respond to whatever you communicate to it. For example, have you ever wished ill or anger to someone, only to stub your toe, bang

your head, cut your finger on the bread knife, or create some other expression of self-inflicted pain? Similarly, have you ever felt quietly lucky about something and it comes up trumps for you? Have you ever thought how nice it'd be to have a certain thing in your life and some time later you get it?

Watching Your Emotions

People whisperers appreciate the wonderful gift of emotions and their ability to enhance or detract from communications and relationships. People whisperers observe their own emotions with interest, so they come to know themselves better and become more successful at relating with other people.

There are a huge range of emotions that we can experience as human beings and they are more often than not triggered by another person or people in our lives. Certain people seem to have the ability to set off more powerful emotions in us than other people; and it is often those that are closest to us who can do that. Some emotions are powerful and intense, some are gentle, some enjoyable and some decidedly unpleasant! A big part of listening to yourself involves listening to your emotions.

Exploring your emotions ...
Who decides how you feel?
Who is in control of your emotions: you or someone else?
Are you in control of your emotions or are they in control of you?
Do your emotions ever "run away with you"?
Do you like feeling all the emotions you feel?
What or who causes you to feel strong emotions?
Do your emotions ever get in the way of your enjoyment in your relationships?
For you to have a more fulfilled life, which emotions would you like to have more of?
For you to have a more fulfilled life, which emotions would you like to have less of?

If you lived alone on a desert island, you might feel emotions such as loneliness, fear, desperation or the hope of being rescued by a passing ship, but living fully in the flow of society, relationships, work and all that goes with them, you can certainly feel some stuff! And some of it can be very challenging.

In the course of just one day you might feel love for your partner or family, miserable at having to get out of bed, depressed that it is raining, pleased because someone flirted with you, angry because someone let you down, frustrated at sitting in traffic, uplifted by a great song on the radio, happy to be welcomed home with a smile . . . the list goes on and on and on! The extraordinary thing is that this almost constant stream of emotions goes unnoticed most of the time; you just carry on living with the constant background noise of changing emotions playing away inside of you.

We can become addicted to feeling certain emotions and start seeking them out as though they are some kind of drug.

RIDING THE ROLLER COASTER

When life is like an emotional roller coaster it can use up a huge amount of energy and cause you react to other people in ways that harm your relationships, but you can make the roller-coaster ride easier by simply observing your emotions.

When you notice an emotion as you feel it, you effectively change what is happening for you. Instead of being hauled along on the roller coaster of the emotion, you watch it like an observer, while still feeling and expressing it at the same time.

For example, if you were exasperated by someone close, you might watch your heated feelings and think, "Hmm, that's interesting, look how angry I am feeling about that!" Or maybe you are excited when someone you find attractive walks in the room:

you might notice your pulse start racing and your head go fuzzy and think, "Wow, what a warm glow I am getting when I'm near that person!"

Life without emotion could be very dull:
life with too much emotion can be exhausting.

WHOSE EMOTIONS ARE THEY?

Nearly everything you do in life relates to other people, but that still doesn't give them or you the right to choose how each other should feel . . . you probably wouldn't let your neighbor choose the color of your sofa (maybe you would) or a work colleague choose a spouse for you, but you may well allow someone else to choose how you feel! And the crazy thing is: we all do it and think that it is normal!

It is not for you to decide how to make other people feel or for them to be responsible for how you feel. This can be a hard thing to accept, especially if you think that someone you care about is making you feel low, lonely or useless, for example.

EMOTIONS CAN MOTIVATE OR LIMIT

Some emotions are fantastic for getting people into action: great speakers throughout history have aroused their followers' emotions in times of war, for example. You can use the kind of emotions that excite you to achieve more and move forward in life to great advantage, as well as making you a more inspiring and easier person to be around.

Not all emotions or emotional reactions are helpful and some can positively hold you back from being who you really are. They can also stop you from connecting with other people in the way you would like to.

What emotions do you experience that stop you from doing the things you dream of?

How would your life be if you didn't experience those limiting emotions?

Do you know someone who doesn't have those same limiting emotions as you? What do they do instead?

Who gave you those limiting emotions in the first place?

What would you rather feel instead?

Ask yourself: who or what chooses how I feel?

HABITUAL EMOTIONS

✦ Do you habitually experience any particular types of emotion? Do you often feel angry, frustrated, afraid or needy? If this is happening to you, begin to notice what patterns are running and what triggers the habitual emotion. Remember that merely recognizing the pattern is the first step toward liberating yourself from it.

✦ How might you benefit or how might you lose by allowing yourself to experience emotions habitually?

✦ Whenever the emotion arises, notice it with objective interest, like a zoologist observing interesting behavior in an animal through binoculars. Noticing when something arises is a way of breaking the hold it has over you.

EXTREME EMOTIONS

If extreme emotions are stirred up, it is impossible to ignore them. We all know that emotions can be very powerful: they can make a man die for love; they can make people kill in anger; they can make nations turn into genocidal maniacs.

Let's face it, when you are overwhelmed by feelings of being in love, seething with anger, feeling overwhelmed with joy, or paralyzed by fear, you have no chance of pretending it is not happening to you!

As long as they are not going to harm anyone, it is sometimes best to allow extreme emotions to come up and run their course, rather than attempting to contain them. If you can observe your emotions at the same time as feeling them, then you really are on the way to becoming a people whisperer.

Things to do:
1. Observe how you feel!
2. Start to notice what sets you off into particular emotional states.
3. Take on board the idea that no one else can really make you feel a certain way without you giving them permission.
4. Notice which emotions enhance your relationships. Notice which emotions detract from those relationships. Which emotions are particularly pleasurable? Which are overwhelming or potentially destructive?
5. Watch other people and see how their emotions either improve or spoil their relationships.
6. Be aware when extreme negative emotions are running away with you. Allow them to run their course in a safe way, but continue to consciously notice what is happening.

Fear and Guilt

People whisperers understand how the powerful emotions of fear and guilt can interfere with the flow of joy in our communications. There may be people who can *make* you feel fear and those who can *make* you feel guilt. Even worse than that: there are probably people in your life who will try to make you feel fear or guilt for their own ends, to derive energy from you or to gain control or power over you.

Fear and guilt are two ways to communicate with yourself that can make life quite uncomfortable. It may not be easy, but every time you feel fear or guilt you do have a choice as to whether you allow it to control you or not. The type of fear we are talking about here is not physiological—such as the fear of being eaten by a lion if, by some bizarre set of circumstances, you find yourself in the lion's enclosure at the zoo!

Fear is an anxious state created by the anticipation of pain or hurt: it may be that the pain or hurt doesn't actually happen, but we have still harmed ourselves and used our energy by feeling the fear of it psychologically.

It is not uncommon for us to be afraid of someone hurting us or reacting in a way that we would find frightening. Unfortunately, our fears "inter-fear" with our behavior and how we act around people, which can hold us back from experiencing good relationships with them.

It is important to acknowledge fear when it is present: by acknowledging it you shine light onto it.
The light can then show you the way forward.

MANAGING FEAR

Another word for "managing fear" is "courage." Fear is not always something we can remove from a situation, but what we can do is find ways to function despite the fear; and that requires courage.

If you feel yourself becoming fearful or anxious about a particular person, meeting or interaction, wait and take time to settle yourself inside, observe the breath going in and out of your body and allow yourself to find your peaceful "center" before taking action.

FEAR THAT BLOCKS COMMUNICATION

When it comes to communicating with other people, our fears can stand in the way of us saying what we think or feel, or what needs to be said. We fear how the other person may react if we say what we would like to say, so instead of expressing it, we hold back. Sometimes this may be a wise thing to do, but sometimes things need to be expressed for the sake of truth, clarity and openness.

Often, our fear of how someone is going to react is far greater than their actual reaction. If you can let someone know that you are only voicing how you feel and not necessarily airing opinions about them, you may find it easier to say your piece, since the person you are talking to will know they are not on the receiving end of a personal criticism.

✦ What things might you have done in your life if fear hadn't stopped you?

✦ What things might you do or say if fear were not stopping you now?

✦ What would you do with the rest of your life if there were no fear?

✦ Do you ever find yourself not communicating to your loved one for fear of saying or doing the wrong thing?

✦ Do you ever find yourself implying what you need to say to someone, rather than saying it in a clear, straightforward way: as though you are trying to say it, but hiding it at the same time?

FREEDOM FROM GUILT

The power of guilt to dominate and control people has long been recognized as a useful weapon by some societies and organized religions: they have often used it not to control or overpower their enemies, but, bizarrely, to hold power over their own followers.

Guilt has been created by people to control people. Nature doesn't feel guilt. When a leopard kills a zebra, when a whale scoops up a whole shoal of fish in one mouthful, when a savage winter ravages the countryside, even when a fox kills every bird in the hen-house then only eats one of them, nature doesn't indulge in feeling guilty and saying "Oh, I'm so bad." It keeps moving forward and continues to create more incredible beauty and abundance.

WHO IS MAKING YOU FEEL GUILTY?

Guilt is another limiting way that we communicate with ourselves. In truth, you are the only one who can make you feel guilty—no one else can do the job for you. Other people can say things in an attempt to trigger your feelings of guilt, but they cannot make you feel guilty unless you allow them to.

If you feel guilty about things you have said or done, perhaps now would be a good time to tell yourself that nobody is perfect and we all do or say things that aren't ideal sometimes. While it may be a constructive thing to recognize when you have done something unreasonable, harmful or thoughtless, it is not constructive to keep replaying it and beating yourself up over it forever. As you give yourself permission not to feel guilty, it will be less easy for people to control you by pressing your "guilt buttons," since the buttons will not trigger a reaction any more.

Are there people who you think ought to feel guilty about things they have said or done to you? If you think someone should feel guilty for something they said or did to you, it isn't really doing them any harm, but *it is doing you harm*. What would it take for you to let them off the hook?

Things to do:
1. Explore your fears: think of people or situations you have feared in the past and that turned out to be fine.

2. If there is someone you are afraid of, try putting yourself in their position and seeing if you can understand what makes them behave in a way that scares you. Could it be that they themselves are terrified of something?

3. When fear comes up in you, accept that it is there and watch it with objective fascination, like you would watch a small woodland creature that has come out from the shrubbery!

4. Write down the things you feel guilty about and how long you think it would be constructive to continue beating yourself up about it. Then next to each thing, write down what positive benefit you gain from feeling guilty about it. Now do what nature does: drop the guilt and move forward to a new day and the coming of the next season.

5. Become observant of how other people use fear and/or guilt to control you: once you see how this is happening, you have a conscious choice about whether or not to allow them to continue controlling you with fear and guilt, even if you have to take the drastic measure of removing them from your life or removing yourself from theirs.

6. Write a list of all the people you think should feel guilty for what they did to you. If you can, think of a positive reason why they might have done what they did to you. Think of something you may have learned from their treatment of you. Their past behavior now only exists in your memory. In your mind, thank them, tell them you forgive them and that it is now time for you to let them go.

In this second secret we have explored how to listen to yourself through your thoughts and feelings and seen how the ways you communicate with yourself affect your whole life and especially your relationships with other people. We have learned that just by noticing your thoughts and feelings, without attempting to alter anything, you can expand your people whispering skills. Secret Three will take this exploration even further, by making use of one of your most precious gifts: your body.

SECRET THREE
Trust Your Body

I was in the riding arena with Arania, a sensitive young Spanish mare. I have worked on the ground beside her until there is calmness and trust between us, as I had done with many young horses before her. But at some point I would have to go to a place where no other human has ever gone before, and that is on this horse's back for the very first time. How and when I chose to sit on her for the first time mattered as much to her as it did to me. If I did it at the wrong time or in the wrong way she might be afraid of being ridden for a long time, and I might end up getting badly hurt. For a human to climb onto a horse's back for the first time is contrary to the instincts of both creatures. The horse is a prey animal, so allowing a predator such as a human to climb on him or her is akin to a zebra allowing a lion to climb on its back. The human is equally vulnerable: giving up his connection with the ground means risking his survival.

People rightly say that horse whispering has a lot to do with body language and horses communicate mostly with their bodies. This fact is true, but as my work with horses went deeper, I realized that my own body, as well as the horse's body, was a source of much information and more than just by external physical movements. Working with unbroken horses showed me that the internal state of the body and its surrounding energy field that tells us how others feel. It also tells us how we feel and what the right course of action to take is. What was amazing about this realization was the fact that if I listened to my body, it never lied.

So how could I *know* when and how it was right to ride Arania for the first time? Experience has taught me that if I listen well enough to my body, I can trust that it will guide me to do what is right. If I notice my heart beat faster than normal, my legs feel shaky or my throat is dry, then it is probably not OK to ride the horse, because the horse will sense my fear and become afraid too. If my body feels completely peaceful inside and out, then it is probably OK to climb on the horse's back. Of the countless times I have backed (ridden) young horses for the first time and my body told me it was OK, it has been a peaceful, stress-free experience for me and the horses. When my body said it wasn't OK and for one reason or another I didn't listen, I have frightened the young horse and taken the consequences by being hurt myself.

With Arania on that particular day, my body and my breathing were calm and unflustered by the idea of sitting upon her for the first time. I stroked her neck and back where I intended to sit. She was intrigued and watched me trustingly out of her left eye. I hopped up and down by her side a few times and then over her back so that I lay with my belly across her sideways. She shifted her feet around a little to readjust her balance under my unfamiliar weight, but didn't move off. I continued stroking her neck for a minute or so, and then slowly swung my right leg over her back until I was astride her, quietly raising my torso to sit up bareback on this beautiful horse for the first time. I could feel her slow breath and the warmth of her body underneath me. In that position, both the horse and I were totally trusting and totally vulnerable. I stroked her neck again and looked ahead between her ears out at the world from a place where no one had ever looked: from upon her back. The level of mutual trust and the sacredness of the moment we shared made my chest want to explode with joy.

People whisperers know that your body is one of the greatest allies you can have. They are aware that your body is an inte-

gral and physical manifestation of who you are and that it constantly guides you toward the right course of action.

Our bodies give us constant, moment to moment feedback about how we feel, what we think and the way we are interacting with our environment and the people in it. Unfortunately, we only really listen to our bodies when they start giving us information we cannot ignore, normally in the form of aches, pains, disease, bursts of joy or sexual excitement. The rest of the time our bodies are doing their best to tell us what is going on but we rarely listen.

Your body is a part of who you are and is always
looking out for you; whispering information that will guide you,
if you are able to listen.

WHAT IS YOUR BODY TELLING YOU?

Trusting your body and listening to the whispers of information it is giving you is a key part of communicating with yourself. Every cell in your body reflects your thoughts and emotions: it is a fabulous source of information about what is happening in your life and how you feel about the people around you. Your body effectively carries a blueprint of all you have ever thought, felt or experienced.

Feedback is being given to you by your body in every single exchange you have with other people. This information can help you to find your way through life and guide you to interact with the right people in the right way, for your benefit and theirs. The information your body gives you can act like an early warning radar, helping you to avoid situations, people or relationships that may become too hazardous or difficult.

Like the skin of a chameleon that changes color in response to its environment, your body changes in response to your environment too. Have you ever noticed how some people *make* you feel uncomfortable and others *make* you feel comfortable? This is an example of your body giving you feedback. Other ways your body gives you feedback are by telling you what types of food are right for you or what exercise is appropriate.

THE BODY DOES NOT LIE

Unlike our minds and our mouths, which can lie even to us, the body responds at a deeper and more honest level. You may tell yourself, for example, that you don't feel anxious about discussing a particular subject with someone, but your body will know the truth and have the "butterflies" regardless of what your mind says. You may tell yourself that you don't find a particular person physically attractive, and if that isn't true, your body will certainly inform you otherwise!

It is important to realize that your body is giving you feedback the whole time, not just in major situations. The different ways your body reacts are often very subtle, but if you are aware of those reactions, you can use the information to guide your communications with other people.

Here are a few ways our bodies can give us feedback:

✦ When we feel insecure, unsafe or defensive our bodies tend to "close up." We cross our legs, fold our chest in a little, drop our eyes away from the other person and fold our arms across our chest. Internally our joints and muscles may tighten slightly, the heart beats faster and breathing becomes shallower and the stomach (solar plexus) tightens.

✦ If we are anxious or nervous in certain situations or with particular people the stomach can churn, the body increases in tension ready for fight or flight, we can feel sick, the throat closes slightly, our legs can feel wobbly, our eyes flit about or look tight and startled and the bowels may feel looser (hopefully not too loose!).

✦ Feeling comfortable or loving toward someone causes the whole body to feel more at ease. The stomach, muscles and joints release, the chest opens (in eastern tradition this is the heart chakra opening), we take on a relaxed and friendly posture, "spread out," take up more space and have soft eyes.

✦ Feeling excited or full of fun can create a sense of the body expanding; the face opens (literally in smiles and laughter), we feel lighter and our body moves with more freedom and release. We can also feel the heart beating faster, but in a healthy aerobic way, rather than pumping the fight or flight hormone, epinephrine, round our body.

✦ If the person you are with makes you feel sexually excited, well, hopefully you've noticed what your body feels like in that situation already!

Three Key Questions to Ask Yourself:
1. What is my body telling me right now?
2. What is my body telling other people right now?
3. What are other people's bodies telling me?

TUNE IN TO YOUR BODY

Every single thought creates a reaction in your body. To become aware of this, sit comfortably and quietly with your eyes closed and think of someone or something that you find really relaxing and peaceful. Feel how your body softens and relaxes, your heart slows, your stomach lets go. Now think of a person or situation you have to face that is scary or challenging . . . What happens to your body? Most likely it starts getting tense, your stomach knots and heart rate speeds up.

ACKNOWLEDGING THE FEELING

The same as with people whisperer Secret Two (when we explored thoughts and emotions), simply noticing your body's reactions and acknowledging the messages will help you to manage situations better.

If you give your body your attention as though you are an interested onlooker, you take some of the power out of your reaction. By paying attention and trusting your body, you gain more control over situations, and then have a choice of whether to respond or react.

If your body has to scream at you before you take notice of it, the state it is in will make the situation worse, by making you more tense, angry or frightened, for example.

If you listen to your body when you are with other people,
it will tell you a great deal about them.
It may tell you whether they are being honest or not.

FIONA'S STORY

To begin with, Fiona loved her new job: not only did she enjoy what she did, but it gave her the opportunity to live in the countryside, since the post she had found came with a cottage attached. She was also able to keep her horse there, and it was the first time she had ever been in such a lucky position. Fiona didn't even have to travel to work any more: because her employer's home, the main house on the estate, was the center for his business. It all seemed to fit perfectly.

From time to time through her life, Fiona had experienced bouts of eczema and asthma. When I first met her she had been in her new job for about three months, by which time her eczema and asthma had reappeared and were becoming increasingly worse. Before long, she was in constant discomfort and forced to seek the advice of specialists. As well as following a very pure diet, she was given a prescription to control her raging symptoms, but nothing appeared to work. It seemed more than coincidental that her ailments had worsened so significantly since moving to her new place and job, and so I asked Fiona if perhaps her body was trying to tell her something.

Fiona is a very amenable, gentle and sensitive person, in stark contrast to her employer, who was sometimes very difficult to deal with. He was a loud, controlling, even bullying man, who would fly off the handle at the slightest upset, not caring what he said or who was on the receiving end of his tantrums. After putting up with this for nearly two years, Fiona had become quite worn out by tiptoeing her way through the daily minefield created by this atmosphere of fear and intimidation, and so she finally found another job to go to.

Within days of moving away from her old job and home, Fiona experienced an almost miraculous recovery from her eczema and asthma. It has been said that eczema is caused by intense irritation and that asthma is caused by things being suppressed and not said. Both of these descriptions fitted perfectly with Fiona's situation. Fearing the temperamental reactions of her boss, she had constantly suppressed what she wanted to say and, as a consequence, she lived in a state of permanent irritation. Had Fiona listened to her body sooner, she may have realized that her body was shouting a message to her, telling her the situation she had placed herself in was not good for her and she ought to get out of it. Her body had been letting her know for nearly two years that she needed to move away, and thankfully she eventually listened. These days Fiona often mentions the messages she ignored at that time and now listens very attentively to her body at all times.

Things to do:

1. Stop reading for a moment and scan your attention down through your body. Start with your head: how do your scalp, jaw and tongue feel? Now check your neck, shoulders, guts, lower

spine, seat, legs and arms. Are there any pockets of tension that you hadn't been aware of? Can you release them?

2. Sit comfortably and quietly and think of a person or situation you are really anxious or frightened about. Listen to what your body tells you, even in response to merely thinking about the person or situation. Repeat this process until you can think vividly about the person or situation without your body reacting at all.

3. Allow your body to be really relaxed and then think in depth about various people in your life, one at a time. See what your body tells you in response to thoughts about different people.

4. See if you can become aware of your whole body as a complete entity. Stay with this for a moment and be aware of how it feels.

5. Next time you are talking to someone, bring your awareness into your body while the conversation is happening: scan through it to see what it is doing or feeling.

WATCH YOUR BODY TALK

As well being a great source of information for you, your body also plays a large part in communicating with other people. Opinions vary, but it is generally agreed that less than fifty percent of communication happens via the spoken word. People whisperers are aware of the messages communicated via body language, their own and others', and by being aware of body language, they "hear" much more than just the spoken word.

As we have already seen, your body, thoughts and emotions are all intimately linked. As well as your body being influenced by your thoughts and emotions, you can also turn things around and use your body to influence your thoughts and emotions. By changing what you do with your body, it is possible to change your emotions and the way you feel, and to change what you are communicating to other people.

If you take up a dominant and powerful stance with your body (like Arnie Schwarzenegger in the movie *Terminator*) it can make you feel more powerful and solid in yourself, even though other people may snigger!

If you take up a body posture that is timid and closed, you will feel that way.

If you wave your arms in the air, smile and dance around, it is almost impossible to feel miserable.

INFINITE WAYS TO EXPRESS

Your body-talk influences the nature of every communication you have with yourself and with other people. Once you listen and become aware of what your body is communicating, there are infinite ways you can use it to express yourself.

- To appear nonchalant, take up a casual, open posture, sighing and focusing on inner relaxation.
- To appear determined, take up a firm stance and feel more solid inside and out.
- To appear unthreatening, allow softness into your face and body, rest one leg and center yourself inwardly.
- To appear completely unstoppable, focus your eyes to the horizon, become firm but not fixed inside and raise yourself up.
- To project an air of unconditional love and acceptance (very worthwhile in many situations), relax your stomach muscles and take gentle, slow breaths. Give your full attention to the other person, let your mind and body be still and feel centered in your torso.

Learning to use your body and postures consciously can seem strange to begin with, but all of the body language you already use is learned, you weren't born with it. Proof of this can be seen in the way teenagers acquire a different way of standing and moving when they hang around with other teenagers on the block. What was a perfectly good posture and walk for a child is uncool for a teen; they have to learn to walk like the latest movie star or rapper dude.

The dictionary is full of words we rarely use. Likewise there are many physical expressions our bodies are capable of that we don't normally use. Extending your "body-language vocabulary" is the same as learning to use new words: speaking new words feels strange until we integrate them into our everyday vocabulary, and in the beginning we sometimes use them in the wrong context (much to the amusement of others).

THE POWER IN YOUR BODY

Your external body language expresses messages to others, but what can make those expressions really powerful is if your internal emotional "state" matches your external body language: when you feel the same inside as your body shows on the outside, your communication becomes highly expressive and focused.

Your body is most powerful when it is fully aligned with your thoughts, intentions and emotions. Your actions become highly effective and your body becomes a fantastic tool for expression, so you can give apparently tiny signals and get big results. It follows that when your body is not aligned with the rest of you, even performing huge effortful actions with your body have little or no effect.

"Alignment" means that your mind, body and whole intention are in agreement: all these parts of you think, aim and believe in exactly the same thing. Your body then becomes the physical manifestation, the tip of the iceberg, of all those inner resources in action. This is how great athletes can achieve such feats (apart from having incredibly athletic bodies!); their body is powered by the mind, focused intention and inner energy and expresses it with such commitment that the results can be outstanding.

You can use the same level of alignment to perform feats of incredible stillness too; your body becomes a physical representation of inner stillness and peace, so that it appears you are untouchable. This can have a very calming effect on heated situations, almost as though your body is a fire blanket, damping down the flames of the exchange.

When you speak with alignment,
your body naturally supports your message.

PEOPLE WATCHING

Noticing other people's body language can help a great deal: you can often tell how someone feels or what they are thinking by observing their posture and body-talk. When someone's body tells you how they feel, you have more idea about what might be the right thing to say to them at that time (or whether it may be wiser to keep quiet and not say anything).

THERE ARE MANY SUBTLE MESSAGES YOU CAN SEE BY WATCHING SOMEONE'S BODY-TALK . . .

✦ Watch someone's eyes while they talk. Watch their eyes change as the things they talk about change. Do their eyes shine out with light or are they dull? Do their eyes flit about or are they restful and able to look at you? Do their eyes convey love or mistrust? The eyes are said to be the windows of the soul. When you look into someone's eyes, what do you see of them?

✦ Is their mouth and jaw relaxed or tight? Do they open their mouth and speak their truth freely or do they talk through a half-closed mouth, as though their words don't matter or are maybe not true? When they smile, do their eyes smile along with their mouth or do they not give much away?

✦ Watch how someone sits, stands and moves, what they do with their body mass. Do they move in a centered or apologetic way, in a nervous or confident way, calmly or with agitation? Does their head and shoulder position look light and floating or heavy and weighed down by life? Do their shoulders look rounded and worn or proud and strong? What speed are their movements? Do they have to fiddle with things and keep adjusting themselves or do they have a comfortable inner stillness about them?

THE AURA

We could explore external body language for a long time, but there is another level at which we can listen to another person's body; the subliminal presence and energy that someone brings with them when they enter a room, the "atmosphere" they carry within and around them. Some people may call this the "aura." I can't say whether auras exist in the literal sense (I've never seen one but that doesn't mean they aren't there!), but however skeptical you may be about them, every person you meet definitely has a different kind of energy surrounding them. This energy, feeling, aura or whatever you want to call it is quite tangible most of the time and is a valuable source of information for us in our communications with other people. A people whisperer certainly stays open and trusts what their body tells them about the aura or energy field of other people.

Things to do:

1. Explore ways to support your communications by using your body in different ways, using the suggestions in this chapter. For example, practice having a "bigger," louder physical presence and then having a "smaller," quieter physical presence. Notice how changing your body language affects your emotions or self-confidence levels.

2. Start to notice how you walk, stand and sit. What does your posture say about you? Is your body language open or closed, receptive or intimidating?

3. Pay attention to what people do with their facial expressions, hands and body when they are talking to you. Pay attention to what your face, hands and body do when you are talking to them.

4. Stand and look at yourself in a full-length mirror. What stance do you naturally take? If you met someone with your posture, what kind of person would you guess they were? Play around with the variety of ways you can express with your body. See how tiny changes in the mirror make a real difference to what is being expressed.

5. Next time you are talking to someone, allow your subtle "inner" body or aura to listen to the other person's subtle inner body. What kind of experience does that give you?

In the first three secrets of the people whisperer, you have discovered how you communicate with yourself through your thoughts and emotions and by being who you really are. You have seen what a great ally and source of information your body is and you have looked at how other people's bodies communicate with you in various ways. In the next four secrets, you will gain insights into developing your relationships and loving communications with the people in your life.

PART II

Whispering
to Others

SECRET FOUR
Hold the Space

I am riding a stunning Lipizzaner horse out across miles of open moorland for the second consecutive day and feeling pleased with myself about how well he is going: he is listening to me and even stepping out in front of the other horses, which I am told he would not normally do.

This horse has a lot of "problems" and is quite untrained. Before he came to us, he had been a driving horse and was driven alone on roads pulling a carriage too soon in his training. One time he had taken fright, bolted down a lane and fallen into a ditch with the carriage upside down on top of him. As a consequence of this and various other unpleasant experiences in his early life, people talked about him being a very nervous ride and a horse that didn't "listen" to his rider's directions very much.

So now I am riding this impeccably well-behaved Lipizzaner horse, gazing out across the endless beautiful landscape and perfect blue sky and feeling good about the way my training of him is progressing so quickly and wondering why people had found him challenging. That all changes in less than a moment and much faster than I can think: he spins around and gallops for home. My unbuttoned coat flaps as a result of his sudden movement, increasing his panic as he attempts to flee from the flapping "coat monster" he now perceives is on his back. He instinctively bucks repeatedly to rid himself of my flapping coat, which I am still wearing, until he dislodges me. My coat and I land with a thump on the ground and he disappears into the yonder.

I limp stiffly home across the moorland, expecting the horse to be standing waiting at the entrance to the stable yard, which is entered via a cattle grid (a type of grille laid across the road to stop animals). He is not there. In fact he is already in the stable yard where, I am told, he landed after jumping clean over the cattle grid in sheer terror.

As I think back to what happened, I wonder whether I could have anticipated and averted the incident. My question is answered by a humbling and unwelcome observation from one of my companions, who says she wondered why I had taken him out in front like that and pushed him when he looked so obviously worried and uncomfortable. Ouch. I guess I hadn't been really listening to him!

After suffering quite a few hard knocks from horses, I began to realize that horse whispering is less about making horses do things and more about "listening" to what they are expressing via their body language, actions, attitude, emotional state and energy levels.

It seems that being open to really listening to what a horse or a person is experiencing or feeling is often enough to build a successful partnership or solve a problem: and it saves us from taking any more hard knocks! Horses, like people, actually express themselves in one way or another constantly, and yet humans are so often ambushed by a horse's apparently unexpected behavior, this despite the fact that ninety-nine times out of one hundred, the horse has communicated a warning for quite some time. Unfortunately, I wasn't listening to the horse's warnings until it expressed them in a major and potentially dangerous way.

"Listening" to horses obviously has nothing to do with listening to speech; it is "listening" with your body and being totally open to whatever feedback, emotions or responses are being expressed by the horse. The great thing is that this way of listening is something that can be equally wonderful when applied to people.

People whisperers are aware at every level—mentally, emotionally and physically. This awareness applies to all forms of communication, but especially in the quality of the way that they listen. They know that the ultimate form of listening is the loving gift of "holding the space."

Holding the space means you listen to someone by being totally present; it means giving them your heart, love and full attention. This allows them all the room they need to express themselves. You stay in a peaceful state and create stillness around you and allow the other person to express whatever they wish to express, or say whatever they need to say. You don't analyze, judge or try to find solutions. When you hold the space you really do listen to the whole of them with the whole of you, which means you listen to their energy and essence, as well as to the words they use.

When you hold the space it is all about the other person. You are giving them love and respect by being fully there and not attempting to take up any of the space with your own ego or "stuff." You lay aside all of your own worries, ideas, expectations, wants and thoughts for the duration of the time that you are with the other person in this listening mode.

Holding the space and giving someone your full attention inside and out is one of the greatest gifts you can give.

QUESTIONS FROM BEYOND THE MIND

When you ask questions while holding the space, the questions do not come from your mind, they come from your intuition. You do not think about the question before you ask it, the question somehow comes out of what the other person has previously said. This way, if you do ask questions, they are always the right ones. Sometimes when you hold the space you may even ask questions that surprise you as you say them.

THE GIFTS OF HOLDING THE SPACE

✦ Holding the space allows all kinds of incredible realizations to come about, for you as well as for the other person.

✦ Holding the space quite simply allows for expansion: quite simply, because you are creating more space.

✦ Holding the space makes someone feel totally safe to explore and say whatever they want without fear of reaction; it is almost as though you hold them in a protective bubble where there is only them, you and the area surrounding you both. They are protected from anything outside of the bubble and everything inside is totally non-judgmental and safe.

✦ Holding the space is the ultimate in high-quality listening because nothing else is going on within you except that. This is what makes it such high-quality listening.

✦ Holding the space often brings about great solutions or learning for someone, but in one sense you have not had to *do* anything. You have just been totally there: with your love and an open heart.

The opposite of holding the space is what we do most of the time. We fill every corner of time and space in our lives with business, with our own stuff—with talking, thinking, wanting, pushing, wishing, etc. The space is always there for us to expand into, it is just that we fill it up all the time. Like concreting over the earth, it is there everywhere underneath, but we cover it up.

Things to do:

1. Practice being aware of your own inner space: the space taken up by your body and the near surrounding area. Practice being totally quiet, inside and out.

2. Allow someone to express themselves while you give your full, loving, undivided attention. Acknowledge their view and accept that their reality is their reality, whether it contrasts with yours or not.

3. Enjoy the two-way feeling of energy that happens when you hold the space for someone. As you allow them the space to expand, you too are inevitably expanded, since you are an integral part of what is happening.

Truly Listening

Listening really is one of the foundation stones of successful communications and relationships. To truly listen means to absorb what someone is saying with your whole self—body, mind and soul. Truly listening is one of the ultimate loving acts you can perform and one of the most powerful forms of exchange that can take place between people.

When you truly listen to someone, you give them a gift beyond words. Truly listening gives someone a safe space in which to express themselves; it helps them to see things in ways they never saw before, or to explore areas of themselves and their lives that they haven't done before. Sometimes people just need to talk, to be free to offload whatever is going on for them, and in this way, truly listening can be like healing given by the listener to the person talking.

15 TIPS FOR TRULY LISTENING:

1. Have an attitude of infinite patience.
2. Don't interject with comments to prove that you are listening.
3. Give love by allowing the other person to express who they really are.
4. Don't try to "fix it for them" by coming up with solutions to their dilemmas: only they can discover the solutions that are most appropriate for them. Your listening will help them in their discovery.
5. Avoid giving your opinion or telling someone what they should, shouldn't or ought to do.

6. Have a quiet mind.

7. Never alter the words or the meaning of the words spoken by someone else.

8. Intuitively know the right question to ask or the right thing to say.

9. Avoid having negative feelings inside you that are "emotionally" opposed to the other person.

10. Absorb far more than what is said by their words alone.

11. Have a sense of the space around you and the other person, almost like you are in an invisible capsule that surrounds and suspends you both.

12. Avoid trying to justify, sort out, compare, judge or discard any of what is said. (That doesn't mean you have to agree with what is being said!)

13. Become so present-moment-focused that you suspend your awareness of time.

14. Don't do anything else at the same time. Put aside everything else and just listen.

15. "Hear" what is being said with your whole self, your whole body, mind and soul—not just with your ears and your brain.

HOW TO LISTEN WITH YOUR BODY

Spoken words that enter through your ears are one way to listen, but you can take the quality of your listening to a deeper level by making your whole body an open, receiving, listening device. Not in words or sounds, but by allowing the body to be still and receiving whatever type of energy comes from the other person. When you are truly listening, it really is as though your whole body is "listening" to the other person.

To listen with your whole body, allow your mind to be quiet and feel as though you are "opening" the front of your body— your heart, chest and stomach—toward the person talking.

(IMPORTANT: If what the other person says is disturbing or may be harmful to you, instead of opening the front of your body, you can consciously close it or have an invisible screen in front of you to protect yourself.)

Things to do:

1. Experiment with truly listening. Sit or stand quietly, and consciously give someone the level of attention and time they need in order to express themselves to you. Use relaxed, physical stillness as a step toward truly listening: when someone is talking to you keep your body still, peaceful and comfortable. Allow your energy level to settle, let go of thinking about the time and give your full attention to the other person.
2. Practice letting go of judgment or internal analyzing when someone speaks to you, as discussed in Secrets One and Two.
3. Be aware of your entire body while someone is speaking to you; feel the energy in your body and how it is responding to what is being communicated.
4. If someone is rambling on and has gone off the subject, ask relevant questions to bring them back on to the course of a constructive communication.

LISTENING TO FEEDBACK (RECEIVING MESSAGES)

Holding the space and listening means not only listening to other people when they talk, but also listening to the feedback you receive in any form and from all areas of your life. "Feedback" is another word for results; the kind of results we receive in the form of information, messages, reactions and events in response to what we put out into the world through our speech and actions. The question is: how much do we hold the space enough to really listen to the information we receive?

We live in the Information Age and receive information constantly—from the universe, from our relationships with other people and from our own internal sources (body, mind and soul).

Listening is a key part of people whispering, because unless we listen to the feedback we receive, how can we know what the right thing to do or say next is?

In our intimate relationships we are constantly receiving feedback about how our partner is feeling; what we do with that information and whether we use it to enhance the union between us or let it divide us is entirely up to us.

Keys to Noticing Feedback

✦ Pay attention to what is happening around you: know that your life, the people, relationships and happenings within it are all feedback about what you are doing and how you are communicating.

✦ You can make it easier to receive feedback by not taking anything personally. Remember that feedback is simply that: feedback. You may be tempted to interpret it as criticism, aggression, flattery or any one of a thousand-and-one labels, but by labeling it, you may alter the original meaning of the message.

✦ Stop denying it! The easiest way to miss valuable feedback is to deny that it is what it is. Everything and anything could be giving you clues that will lead you to the life, relationship, joy, freedom or success you wish for, but if you choose to deny the feedback or refuse to listen, you may miss those gifts.

✦ If someone speaks to you and you are not sure you have understood their meaning, tell them you're not sure what they meant, apologize for not understanding and ask them to express the message again, perhaps in a slightly different way. In 99 percent of cases, this is better than doing too much guesswork and guessing wrongly. Guesswork happens all the time all over the world; it causes lovers to grow apart and races to go to war with each other.

Tiny signals

It is not uncommon for someone in a relationship to "suddenly" be left by their partner without any warning. But is it true there was no warning? Often, people on the outside of the relationship saw it coming because they noticed the tiny signals that suggested it was likely to happen. Sometimes the messages we receive are very quiet, but we still need to hear them. If we are busily wrapped up in our own reality and not listening, it is easy to miss the tiny signals we are being given.

Hear what the universe is telling you through what is happening in your life, relationships and the world around you— even in the tiniest signals.

If we do not listen to feedback, including the small signals, we open ourselves to much bigger, painful or sometimes cataclysmic feedback such as major illness, divorce, bankruptcy or even premature death (in an extreme case!).

Things to do:
1. Try this exercise with a friend: one of you speaks for a little while, then the other repeats back what has been said. The interesting thing is how in the repetition the message will often have been changed so much by the second person.
2. Look at what has happened to you today, yesterday or in the last week and view it as feedback—about decisions you have made, things you have said or done and ways you have been.
3. Look for tiny signals in your life and explore what possible significance they may have.
4. Listen carefully to other people and hear how they filter information in different ways to you. How do they respond to or interpret the same information as you? Use these differences to begin to understand how you filter information and how you might filter it in more helpful ways.

5. Base your decisions and responses on the feedback you receive. Let's face it, the feedback you would get by sticking your hand in a fire would alter your responses very quickly; unfortunately, we don't learn from other sources of feedback in our lives nearly so quickly!

Boomerang Words and Actions

One of the reasons it is important to truly listen to what you say is that every word you speak (and every action you take) will come back to you like a boomerang in some way or other. Every thought, word and action has an energy that goes out from you and will ultimately return to you in some way, although you may not always notice it.

Once you have expressed your words or actions, they are "out there" and once they are out there you have absolutely no control over them—you can only guess how they will come back.

Make thoughtful words and actions one of your routine practices,
because one thoughtless word or action
can undo years of building love and trust.

If you express yourself with love, love will come back to you; if you express yourself with anger, anger will come back. Even when someone is a thousand miles away, if you praise them or wish them well, one day that good intention will come back to you; and if you talk about them in a derogatory way, one day that ill feeling will come back to you.

THE POWER OF WORDS

Once you start to truly listen, it is easy to realize that one of the most amazing communication tools people have is words. Words provide an extraordinary means for us to communicate with each other: they have the power to create or destroy, bring peace or suffering, or love or hate. Not only are there a huge number of words available to us, but each word has so many subtle variations of meaning and inflection, giving us an endless range of possibilities for expression. This allows us to take verbal communication to a very advanced level. Because of the immense power of words, People whisperers truly listen to the words people use and the meanings they convey, both at the conscious and unconscious level.

People whisperers are so aware of the creative and destructive power of words that they choose the words they use with care.

One drawback with the wide variety of possibilities that words present to us is the potential for misunderstanding and misinterpretation; this can be a huge challenge, even in close personal relationships, where two people have found a partner with whom they are extremely harmonious.

The choice of words people use can tell you a great deal about how they operate and what beliefs they have. If you are an aware and careful listener, you can tell quite a lot about someone, even if you have only just met, by noticing their choice of words and how they describe their reality. If you truly listen to the words others use, you will see how their vocabulary is reflected in the kind of life and relationships they create for themselves.

WORDS ARE ALSO A WAY THAT WE COMMUNICATE WITH OURSELVES . . .

One of the things that the people whisperer finds interesting is the unconscious choices we make by the words we use. We often use words habitually, oblivious to the ways those words are holding us back or limiting us.

Remember that your unconscious mind is listening and believing every single word you say. It doesn't take many times of saying things like "I can't" do something, "I am terrible with money" or "I always get my heart broken" before your unconscious mind starts believing it is the truth.

Once the unconscious believes something is the truth, it will affect your behavior in order to bring what it believes to be the truth into reality. This makes your choice of words, even when communicating to yourself, highly significant.

> **Suggestions:**
> Listen to the words you use and realize how they create your reality: remember that words are very powerful so choose them with care.
>
> Read the people whisperer's glossary at the back of this book.

Things to do:

1. Start to notice the words other people use and what they are really saying. Start to notice the words you habitually use and what you are really saying.
2. Begin to notice how words create the experiences, relationships and happenings in people's lives, and even how their words shape and create their personalities. Now think about how your words are shaping you. Start noticing the people who use phrases such as "can't do" a lot and those who use the words "can do" a lot.
3. Listen to yourself and hear the words you are using. You may sometimes be surprised to hear yourself using words that harm you, put yourself down or give you a negative experience. If you notice any of your words doing this, drop them. It may be better to say less than use words that create hurt or negativity in your life or your relationships.
4. Make a commitment to avoid gossiping, especially about other people; remember the boomerang effect, and that words have the power to heal or to harm. Notice how much people bad-mouth those who are not around to defend themselves, and

make a commitment to never criticize or speak negatively about anyone whatsoever, whether they are in the vicinity or not.

5. Start sending positive and loving energy out into the universe through your words and actions. Do this without expecting direct rewards to fly back to you, but watch the results with interest.

6. Whenever someone compliments you, boomerang the gesture back to that person by paying them a compliment in return.

Listening is one of the essential keys to any successful relationship, that's why it is such an important part of people whispering and why we have looked at it in such depth. When you listen so attentively that you "hold the space" for another person, you give them a priceless loving gift.

In the next secret we will look at how to speak with mastery, which means finding ways to say what you want to say, in the confidence that you will be heard and understood.

SECRET FIVE
Speak with Mastery

For about ten years I had a horse-riding center in southwest England where I started (broke in) many young horses. One horse in particular taught me a great deal about communicating in ways that the listener can understand: a beautiful Spanish Andalusian mare, which at four years of age came to me with no name. Because of her over-reactive and extremely neurotic behavior, we called her Bananas. I had never seen a horse with her stunning markings: she had an abundant long mane and her body was very dark gray with bright, white star-bursts. I bought her because I felt sorry for her; she was shut up alone in a stable on a yard where she appeared to have little or no contact with other horses. I have no idea what kind of handling or treatment she had received before she came to me, but suffice to say she was pretty terrified around people and even afraid around other horses.

Over a period of months I tried every method I knew in order to start this youngster and turn her into a riding horse, but whatever I tried she resisted and was determined to teach me something about how I communicated. As time went on I realized her heightened sensitivity meant I had to "speak" to her incredibly quietly, which—since horses read body language—meant the directions I gave her with my body had to be almost invisible. What Bananas gradually forced me to do was look closely at everything I communicated: my tone of voice; the speed and expression of my movements; the way my internal feelings were expressed; my energy level. I needed to be specific in every communication, so all of my messages were crystal clear. If I gave vague or mixed messages her body would tremble and she would attempt to run away in panic. If there was nowhere else to run, Bananas would run straight into the nearest person and knock them down as her means of escape.

This horse was so reactive and afraid that unless I was very understanding, clear, steady and quiet in my communication, she was unable to listen. She demanded that I speak her language or not be heard at all. When I was finally able to connect with her by communicating her way, she opened herself to me and became so trusting, loving and willing that it would bring a lump to my throat and tears to my eyes. What I had done was learned to speak her language: not just the language of horses, but the language of that particular horse, honoring her as a unique individual and in return being honored by being trusted, respected and heard.

When people whisperers communicate, they take responsibility for being understood: to do this they speak with mastery, which means delivering their message in ways that can be easily heard and understood by other people.

If you want to communicate to someone and have them understand you, you have to do it in a way they can understand: it is a waste of time doing it any other way. That may sound like a ridiculously obvious statement, but how many times in life have you spoken to someone and not been correctly understood? If you are anything like me, then probably many times.

Next time you talk to someone, take responsibility for getting that person to understand what you say. This can actually make mundane conversation very interesting—it becomes a little game to find the key to accessing each person's ability to hear you.

10 IDEAS FOR BEING UNDERSTOOD

1. Make it as easy as possible for the listener to hear you.
2. Use vocabulary, words and phrases that your listener knows. To find out what language they understand, get them to do

some talking and notice the words they use, and then use the same ones when talking to them.

3. Make sure you have the other person's attention and be honest with yourself about where their attention is while you talk. You can experiment with getting people's attention in a variety of ways, some more socially acceptable than others! I find painting myself purple and dancing naked on top of the piano works quite well, but it may not be appropriate in every situation. If you want the attention of someone you have a close relationship with, ask them to listen to you for a couple of minutes; this is better than competing with the TV or putting more volume and edge in your voice (which will probably make them withdraw from you further). Sometimes it is best to save your energy: if you realize that you are not succeeding in getting someone's attention, save what you have to say for a time when they are more "available" to listen to you.

4. Say things in different ways until you find the combination that works best for the particular person you are talking to.

5. Speak at a pace that allows them to think about what you are saying. Remember that what you are talking about is familiar to you, but may be totally fresh information for them and they may need time to understand it.

6. Avoid presenting anything in a way that questions or criticizes the person you are talking to. If it sounds like you are criticizing them, their focus will shift from listening to what you are saying to defending themselves, and you will make them unable to hear you.

7. Speak at a volume that can be heard. This is so important. If the listener has to strain to hear because you speak too quietly, they have to work hard to hear your ideas. If you have something worthwhile to communicate, make sure you deliver it at an audible volume, so you sound like you believe in what you say.

8. Make the communication count. Know what you want to say and arrange your words before you speak them, rather than throwing a load of words out into the air like obscure psyche-

delic song lyrics, and then trying to organize them into some kind of meaningful order!

9. Be precise and specific. Avoid being vague or making sweeping generalizations: e.g. "I've seen millions of people do that sort of thing in countless different ways!" You might know what you mean, but if you are vague, the person receiving your ideas may have to do too much guesswork. Most people do not guess accurately, which can lead to misunderstandings and disagreements.

10. If you are asking for something, bite the bullet and ask for it straight. Avoid beating around the bush suggesting what you want and hoping the listener will guess. Make it easy for them.

SPEAKING THE OTHER'S LANGUAGE

One of the key skills in speaking with mastery is the ability to communicate with anyone or anything (horse, dog, cat, alien, etc.) you meet by speaking their language. Among the six billion or so people currently inhabiting the planet there are effectively six billion different languages being spoken, which means speaking a different language with every person you meet. Now that sounds like a challenging task! Everyone has their own personal way of expressing themselves, be it in French, German, English or Swahili.

Speaking the other person's language helps them
to feel recognized, comfortable and understood:
it is done in a very subtle and loving way.

HOW DOES EVERYONE CREATE THEIR OWN LANGUAGE?

We all have a totally unique set of experiences in our lives and unique ways of interpreting those experiences. This is why everyone develops their own way of communicating and why—in order to get the best from our relationships—it helps to speak other people's languages as much as we can.

Speaking another person's language does not mean giving up your own beliefs or agreeing with their values and ideas. It simply means you accept their world-view as being the way they see things (however cock-eyed you might think it is!).

HOW TO SPEAK THE OTHER'S LANGUAGE

Honor how the person feels:

Be open to how someone feels inside. Allow your body to "listen" to their body and notice whatever emotional state they are in. Remember that there is something very giving about making someone "feel" at home in the communication you share with them, which means accepting how they feel. Doing this gives them the sense that you are speaking their language.

Give people space:

Ironically, one of the most effective ways to speak the other's language is to let them do most of the talking! By allowing the other person to talk more, you can listen and learn their language.

You may think you have an important point to get across and can't do that if they do most of the talking, but by listening, learning and then speaking their language, you will get your point across so much more effectively when you do speak.

Ask people questions they want to answer:

Another way to speak the other's language is to ask them questions with interest. This does not mean prying or demanding, just genuinely enquiring into their reality. You can actually work around to asking some very deep and personal questions by following this line of enquiry in a loving way. People can be quite moved when they have the chance to talk about what really matters to them, and will often share far more of themselves with you if you speak their language. This can make them quite vulnerable, which means you have a responsibility to keep the things they say sacred and secret.

Clean language:

Using clean language has nothing to do with swearing. In fact, if the person you are talking to says F*** this and F*** that, it may help them to feel comfortable if you start F-ing along with them!

Everyone has favorite words and phrases they use and feel comfortable with. The same word or phrase can mean different things to different people, e.g. the word "food" can mean "yummy" to one person, "survival" to another and "revulsion" to another.

Clean language means listening to the actual words other people use and then incorporating their same words or phrases when you talk to them.

Mirror body posture and movements:

People express a great deal about themselves and their inner feelings by the way they use their bodies. By and large, our bodies mirror how we feel. By moving in a similar way or taking up a similar posture to the other person, you can unconsciously help them to feel understood. You are essentially speaking their language with your body. What is interesting is how much we do this without even noticing. Next time you stand talking to someone; notice how you are both standing and what you are both doing with your hands.

Touch, sight, sound, smell, taste:

Different people have their own preferences about which of the five senses they use to experience life, and the words they use provide clues as to which of the senses they prefer. Using the same types of words as the other person will help you to connect with them much more effectively.

For example, a person who prefers "touch" might say, "It *feels* like it is going to be a nice *warm* day." Someone who prefers sight might say, "It *looks* like its going to be a *bright* sunny day." Someone who prefers sound might say, "I *hear* it is going to be sunny today: that will *ring* the changes." (Very occasionally you may meet someone who is a "taste" or "smell" type of person, which can be really interesting. I will leave it up to you to play with possible options for words you might use!)

> **Using vocabulary that works**
> ✦ Once you realize someone is a "feeling" or "touch" person, use words like warm, smooth, rough, hold, grip, grasp, handle, etc.
> ✦ Once you realize someone is a visual person, use words like light, dark, picture, vision, see, look, watch, red, blue, black and white, bright, etc.
> ✦ Once you realize someone is an audio person, use words like, ringing, heard, bang, sounds like, tell, voice, speak, hum, etc.

"Toward" and "away from":

Some people are more motivated by moving toward pleasant experiences; others are more motivated by moving away from unpleasant experiences. For example a "toward" person might say, "I love going *to* the coast on holiday and *getting into* the holiday mood." An "away from" person might say, "I love stepping *out* of the rat-race for a while, *getting away* from all the hassle by going on vacation."

Tone and speed:

Notice the tone and speed of the other person's speech and try to match it. If you think about it, it is bound to be easier for you both to get along well if you are talking in a similar way, rather than one of you speaking at the speed of light and high-pitched, while the other speaking s-l-o-w-l-y and deeply.

BEING ADAPTABLE

As we have seen, speaking the other's language basically means being adaptable. It does not mean giving up who you are or flushing your own ideas away. It is not about betraying your own agenda or tricking the other person; it is about honoring their experience of life by speaking their language. It means temporarily adapting the way you say things when talking to someone so that they understand you better. Speaking the other's language should be done in a loving way: if we ever use these methods in a manipulative way, the other person's unconscious will sense it, since it is at that deep level that the most profound communication actually takes place.

Things to do:

1. While remaining true to yourself inside, suspend your own opinions and ideas for a while and experiment with your conversations.

2. Think of speaking the others' language like canoeing across a fast-flowing river: to get to the other side you first need to go with the flow of the river, then gradually guide the canoe over to where you want to be. Enter the stream of someone else's flow by speaking their language, then guide the communication to where you want it to go.

3. Listen with objective interest, not just to what people are saying, but how they are saying it.

MIXED MESSAGES

Giving clear and succinct messages and directions is an important part of speaking with mastery. People whisperers know this means avoiding mixed messages by communicating with absolute focus and clarity. Mixed messages communicate more than one conflicting idea at the same time, on a verbal, physical, emotional or energy level, creating confusion. Mixed messages are everywhere and they can make otherwise ordinary communication give rise to all kinds of difficulties and misunderstandings.

Mixed messages can slow down or hinder relationships between people; because someone receiving a mixed message has to spend time figuring out exactly what was meant.

When you express yourself without mixed messages,
you bring clarity and understanding to your relationships.

When giving out mixed messages, you not only confuse the other person, you also make yourself appear weaker, because what you say is not direct, clear and focused. Mixed messages can make you sound unsure of yourself and diminish your personal power.

Things to do:
1. Listen to the way people speak to each other, especially when making requests. See how they often avoid saying something openly and directly.
2. Look into your own heart and speak honestly, openly and clearly. Ask for what you want: keep it plain and simple.
3. Separate your communications with gaps, so you don't run one message into another and mix them up.
4. Check that you are being "congruent"—that your words, body, heart and mind are sending the same message. If someone does not understand you, check that you are giving a plain, unmixed message.

YOUR TRUE VOICE

The words you use contribute to creating the kind of relationships, communication and experiences you have; but it is not only your words that carry power, it is also the way you use your voice that shapes your life. People whisperers always speak with their "true voice," from a place of respect, integrity, resonance and heart.

Your voice is totally unique. It is a very public expression of who you are. Your voice also expresses *how* you are. Whatever it sounds like, your voice is a beautiful instrument with which you can express yourself.

Through your voice, you interact with other people, not only by the words you use, but by the tone, pitch, speed and emotion with which the sound comes out of your mouth. Your voice also communicates different messages depending on where you speak from inside yourself. Your voice lets people know whether you speak from a place of integrity, insecurity, conviction, truth, untruth, love, bewilderment, confusion, confidence, clarity, insincerity, commitment, strength, tenderness, intimacy or one of many other places within.

The way your voice sounds to the outside world is entirely different to the way it sounds in your head. Have you ever wondered what your voice sounds like to the outside world? Have you ever recorded your voice or heard it played back? What was your reaction? Quite likely it was something like "Oh no, is that my voice? That's not what I sound like is it?" Take the time to listen to the sound of your voice: to notice what its tone, pitch and resonance are like.

People we know well have voices that are instantly recognizable to us: that means in less than a quarter of a second we know who they are and mostly what mood they are in or how they feel. Ask yourself:

◆ Who feels soothed or loved by the sound of your voice?

◆ Who jumps up or feels anxious when you raise your voice?

◆ Who is moved by the sound of your voice?

◆ Who ignores your voice?

◆ Who overpowers your voice with their own voice?

◆ What effect might being told to "keep quiet" have had on you when you were young?

✦ How much do you allow your true voice to come out?

✦ Ask yourself, "What might I be hiding or keeping from the world by not fully opening my mouth and expressing my message?"

SPEAKING WITH YOUR TRUE VOICE

Resonance: Resonance is the breadth and richness to the sound of your voice. People who speak with resonance are allowing the sound to be created within their whole self, like a clear bell. They do not restrict, dampen or pinch the sound; they allow it to ring through their being, so that it is a pleasure to listen to.

Opening your mouth: It may feel strange to open your mouth even a fraction more than usual, but it can make a big difference to how much of your voice is "allowed" out into the world. You may have a voice that could inspire people to greatness, but if it is trapped inside your mouth, the only things to hear the inspiration are your teeth, tongue and tonsils!

The power in your voice: The power in your voice is NOT ABOUT THE VOLUME! It is about where your voice comes from and how much conviction, belief, value and importance you put into what you say. Power in your voice is not something to use to force your way into a conversation or overpower someone else's voice; power is something that is inspiring and interesting, so that when you speak, people listen and hear what you have to say.

Breath—supporting your voice: Your voice is like the tip of the iceberg: it is the part that is in evidence to the outside world, but there is much going on under the surface to support your message. It is the way you use your breath to support your voice that gives the voice its ability to speak from a solid base.

✦ Use your breath to expand your voice, to fill the sails of your words.

✦ Give yourself time and permission to take in the air you need before you speak, so that your voice is held on a cushion of air and therefore sounds lighter, more solid and more comfortable.

✦ Notice where the air needs to go to and come from in your body. Breathe down into your whole body. Explore opening your ribs when you take air in; not just the front of the ribs, but the sides, under your armpits and the back of your ribs.

Speaking with Your Whole Body

Speaking from the heart: When you speak from the heart, your voice carries a message of passion, conviction, belief, truth, compassion and love. When someone is speaking from the heart it can be very moving for the listener. Put your focus on your heart and chest. Allow the feelings you associate with this part of you to come out of your chest; open your heart and trust that it is safe to speak with openness and resonance from this part of you.

Speaking from the head: When someone speaks from the head, they are often analyzing, intellectualizing, rationalizing and expressing thought processes. Speaking from this place is very useful in certain circumstances, as it can help people to understand the mechanics of what is happening and to see their way around problems in a practical way. But there is a danger that you may lose touch with your feelings, and consequently those around you if you speak from the head too much.

Speaking from the stomach/center: This area of the body is the power center. When you speak from here you speak with conviction and centeredness. A voice that comes from this place has a sense of strength, security and belief behind it. Have you ever noticed times when you speak from this place in your body? How is it for you to do that? What effect does it have on those around you? If you don't know how to speak from your power center, think about a subject you feel absolutely clear and strongly about and put your attention on your stomach while you speak. You may be surprised by the power you can produce in speaking this way.

Speaking from the face and nose: Your face is the part of you through which you show most of your expressions to the world. The bones around your cheeks, nose and eyes are a major source of resonance to your voice. If you hold your face in a tight or pinched way, especially the nose, it restricts the ability of your voice to express your true message.

Speaking from the throat: The throat is a very important channel through which your voice comes up from your body and out into the world. If you speak only from your throat, you will restrict the ability of your voice to come from a deeper place.

To speak with mastery, the throat and neck need to be open and relaxed: the first area to tighten when we are tense is often the throat and neck: think how difficult it would be to speak clearly if someone had hold of you around the throat: we often do that to ourselves internally through fear or tension. Relax your throat and neck.

Projecting your voice to where you want it to go

The most effective way to send your voice out into the world is with a clear idea of where you want it to go or who you want to hear it. All too often we talk and just let the words fall out of our mouths and disperse into the ether. If you really believe you are speaking your truth and intend to be heard, think of the direction and distance your voice needs to travel.

If you were firing a water pistol at someone, you would aim it in their direction with a trajectory that would make the water go the right distance. The same simple thing works for your voice.

Speed and pitch

You may notice your voice change its speed and pitch depending on the people or situation in which you find yourself. When you are in a comfortable situation with company that respects and listens to your voice, what is the speed and pitch like? How is it different when you are uncomfortable?

Volume

Sometimes it helps to project your voice, and volume plays a part in that. Sometimes too much volume makes people switch off: their ears take a battering and they quit listening. Sometimes you do need enough volume to reach someone who is a distance away, but volume alone doesn't get a message across.

True volume in your voice comes from a combination of speaking from the right place in your body, resonance and support with the breath. When projecting your voice, allow the volume to come from inside you; give it space and avoid any sense of pushing or *trying* to be loud, as this will create tension in your neck.

Tuning in to Other People's Voices

We have looked at how our voices represent us and reflect our inner state. It is also interesting to notice other people's voices, whether they speak with mastery and how their voices represent them to the outside world.

✦ Does the way other people speak make you feel inspired, bored, strained, excited or interested?
✦ Do they speak slowly or quickly, with resonance or thinly, high pitched or low?
✦ How does the way they speak affect your ability and willingness to give them your attention and hear their message?

When listening to others, it can also be interesting to see if you can tell *where* they are speaking from—the head, heart, body, the forked tongue, or whether they are speaking for someone who is not even present.

Things to do:

1. Listen to the sound of your voice when you speak to different people. When and where do you sound most effective, inviting, secure, inspiring, interesting, clear and communicative?

2. Record yourself speaking. Do this until you feel entirely comfortable listening to your voice!

3. When you are listening to other people speaking, "open" yourself, so that you are truly listening and can feel whereabouts in their body they are speaking from: the heart, throat, head, forked tongue, etc.

4. Practice speaking and directing the sound in a specific direction and at a specific speed toward its destination. Listen to the route the sound takes from your mouth, over to where you wish it to go.

5. When you speak, notice which parts of your face and body resonate or vibrate subtly with the sound. See how releasing or relaxing parts of your body can make your voice sound more full, resonant and powerful.

6. See how different your speech is if you consciously take in just the right amount of air before you begin. Experiment with breathing the air into different parts of your body before speaking and see how even that can change your voice.

To be heard and understood sometimes requires effort: we need to adapt the way we speak so that the listener can hear what we are saying; we need to speak their language and use their words; and we have to experiment with how we use our true voice to be heard. These are all excellent skills to develop along the way.

SECRET SIX
Create Fulfilling Relationships

There have been many times when I have made the mistake of trying to get horses to do things for me by using physical skills, knowledge or my force of will alone. Sometimes such approaches work, but there is a slightly unsatisfactory feeling about getting the result: the horse carries out my wish but the process lacks fulfillment, connection or a feeling that we are doing this "together." Other times, using physical skills and force of will with horses doesn't work at all, and this is when people find they have real problems: they try everything they know to make the horse comply, but if it refuses, there's not a lot they can do except give up and curse the horse for being "difficult."

I remember a time when I was teaching a two-day horseman-ship clinic way up in the north of England and people had trav-eled long distances with their horses to attend. During the clinic a couple of ladies talked at length about how it had taken over three hours to get their big gray "problem" gelding into the trailer before setting off on their journey. They also talked about how they had once taken the horse to a famous horse whisperer's evening demo in order for him to solve the problem of trailer loading. I have a lot of respect for that particular horse whisperer, but by their account it took so long for him to load the horse that most of the audience had either gone home or fallen asleep by the time the horse went in the trailer.

At the end of my clinic people started loading their horses to leave. I said my goodbyes and went back into the arena to give someone a private riding session. When the session was over I returned to the yard to find everyone gone, apart from the two ladies and their big gray gelding. He was sweating, rearing and leaping around the yard and the two ladies were doing the same, but none of them were going anywhere near the trailer!

They asked me to try loading the horse. This big horse was putting out a lot of energy and was scaring the ladies, so I knew I needed to raise my own energy levels to match his. He started taking me quite seriously, realizing I wasn't afraid of his energy like the ladies had been. Thanks to my raised energy, physical knowledge, timing and determination, in a short time he was going half into the trailer. Unfortunately he would go half in and then explosively fly back out again, which he did repeatedly and with a great amount of talent.

Pretty soon I had used up most of my usual ideas and techniques for loading a horse so I stopped to ask myself what I was missing here, what did I need to do differently? I realized that what I was doing was probably what everyone else had done with this horse: they had got hold of the "problem," picked up the rope and used their skills, techniques or whatever else they could think of to get his half-ton body into the trailer, whether he trusted them or not.

Then the penny dropped: what was missing here was love, relationship, acceptance, trust and respect. Even though I was a stranger to this horse, I needed to meet him with love and create a genuine relationship with him. We started again and the next time he went halfway into the trailer. Instead of trying to get him farther in, I just stood and opened my heart to him. I sent him love. In that moment something profound happened between us. Time stood still and I felt a lump in my throat. This magnificent and powerful creature looked at me, his dark soulful eyes softened, and his sides heaved as he took a huge breath and released the fear and tension from his body. He paused and then without any prompting from me walked peacefully toward me and all the way into the trailer. I stroked his huge head, tears in my eyes. The people watching were all crying too.

After a minute or two I led him out of the trailer and back around to the loading ramp. He went softly up the ramp and into the trailer again without hesitation. He went into the trailer with me a few more times, always totally willingly. My heart was bursting. I handed the horse to the owner and he went in with her just as easily.

I didn't speak to the people there about what I had done to enable the horse to make such a radical shift: I didn't fully understand it myself at the time. My guess is we and the horse were all touched by the presence of loving communication that needs no words.

The owner closed the back of the trailer ready to leave and thanked me. I said it was the horse she should thank; he was the one who chose to go into the trailer. She looked at her watch and was surprised to see it had only taken twenty minutes to successfully load her horse—a record time for him by all accounts! Strange how when love comes in, time becomes irrelevant.

People whisperers enjoy fulfilling relationships built on love, approval and healthy exchanges of energy. They are able to create rapport with other people from when they first meet them.

Love and Approval

Expressing love and approval are two of the greatest ways you can connect with others. People whisperers know that we all thrive when we give and receive love and approval.

What We Do for Love

Everything people do in life is motivated by something: everything has a reason behind it that makes us get up and make the effort. Although much of our day-to-day routine is about looking after our basic human needs for survival such as food and shelter, at a deeper level, our interactions with other people are about wanting to be loved. Working to receive love and approval is mostly done unconsciously, but is a very powerful motivator in our lives.

Love that is unconditional, dependable and undemanding,
like the love of a good parent, gives us a strong base
on which to build and live our lives.

Love and Approval Begin with YOU

Many of us are raised to "put others first" or told "it is better to give than to receive." While these phrases may be very charitable, unless you know how to receive, you may not understand how to give to someone else with balance or in a way that they can receive. Many of us may find giving easier than receiving, as being able to receive without resistance requires us to believe we are deserving and "good enough."

Ask yourself:

✦ How much do you love and appreciate yourself? Do you love and appreciate yourself less than the other people in your life? Do you think you are unworthy of being loved and appreciated? Do you feel uncomfortable with the idea of loving yourself?

✦ How often do you compliment yourself on something done well? How do you feel when you or someone else compliments you on something done well?

✦ How do you respond when someone shows you love and approval: by showing thanks and giving love in return, or by feeling awkward and rejecting their gift?

Giving Love and Approval

Giving love doesn't mean going up to people and gushing all over them, although that may be well received in certain company. People have different capacities for receiving love and approval, so people whisperers are sensitive to delivering these gifts in ways that all can receive. One person may need you to be more tactile, another may need you to be less tactile, one may need you to express love in more open ways and one may need you to give love so subtly that it is nothing but a thought sent out on the ether.

HOW DO YOU KNOW THAT SOMEONE HAS RECEIVED YOUR LOVE AND APPROVAL?

Something between them and you will have changed. They will *seem* different. They will look more comfortable within themselves and start reaching out to you. Sometimes you give love and approval to someone and they want to give back to you spontaneously, and sometimes when you put love out, you have to stand back, give them space and wait. Sometimes you simply don't have any sign that the love has been received, but if you know it was given in a way that they could receive, then your part in the process is done.

What someone else does or doesn't do with the love you give is up to them, and you are being even more loving by allowing them the freedom to respond in whatever way they wish . . . even if they don't appear to respond at all.

We all want to be loved and appreciated:
that is the bottom line.

Approval is more than just saying "thanks for doing that job" or "thanks for the coffee"; giving approval is a way of saying "thanks for being who you are and for sharing your time and energy with me." Showing approval to someone when they have reached out to you lets them know you have recognized the energy they have given. Showing too much approval can weaken your position, because it tells the other person you are hungry for their energy and are in danger of "feeding" off them (as we will see explore later).

Resistance to Being Loved and Appreciated

Paradoxically, although one of the most powerful motivators in our lives is the wish to be loved and appreciated, it is very common for us to resist receiving love and appreciation. We can make it hard for people to give us love, praise or thanks, as though we are not worthy. There can be fear attached to being loved and appreciated, almost as though, if we allow someone to help us feel those things, we fear they will gain some kind of ownership of us and be in a position to hurt us or let us down. This is something to bear in mind when your giving of love and approval is not received in an open way.

Resistance to receiving love and approval
can come from a fear of being vulnerable to someone else.

It is easy to think that incredibly self-confident people or those in positions of power, such as people in high positions in corporations, don't need to receive love and approval, but inside they are still human. In fact, leaders and people at the top can find it hard to meet their need for love and approval, since their position means they have to appear so "together" and watertight.

Sometimes, people at the top are only there because they were driven by an unbalanced and over-needy desire to be loved and approved of. Most of us would be happy to be shown love and approval by a few people in our lives: a politician wants the whole population to vote for him or her and give their approval . . . now that IS needy!

The Dance of Giving and Receiving

Once you realize that the wish for love and approval is a universal motivator, you can begin to dance with the flow of love by helping others to meet that need through their connection with you. And as you help others to meet those needs, the positive flow of giving love comes back to you.

It is not healthy to give love and approval with the sole intention of receiving something back from the other person: that would change it from giving into manipulating, and the dance would become a series of contrived, wooden steps.

The gifts we receive in return for giving love and approval are an incidental result of the process, not the reason to do it in the first place.

✦ Remember that universal law always brings back to you what you have given out, so a return gift of love might come from an unexpected source or in a way that you don't expect.

✦ Remember that giving love and approval is an ongoing job, not something to do once or twice and then quit, thinking, "Oh, they already know I love and appreciate them."

Acceptance Is Pure Love

One of the purest ways to give love and approval is to accept someone exactly as they are, with all of their foibles, traits, "faults," habits and ways of being. This is incredibly liberating for people. Once you accept someone totally as they are, they unconsciously know that they are loved, because you are seeing beyond their behavior to the pure "being" underneath.

This opens a whole universe of possibilities, some of which people may find scary. Many of us have never been totally accepted as we are: we are used to not being good enough or truly loved for ourselves. When we are totally accepted: wow! That can be scary . . . it means we are good enough, more than good enough: we are wonderful and lovable.

Ask yourself:

✦ How do the people in your life show you that you are loved?

✦ In what ways would you like them to show you love and approval?

✦ Have you asked them to show you love and approval in a way that they can understand?

✦ How do you show the people in your life that they are loved?

✦ Have you asked them what makes them feel loved by you?

Things to do:

1. What are your five best attributes? Write them down. Now think of five more! Write them down. Now think of five more! Write them down—yes, really do it. Now think of five more! Write them down. Yes, really, really do it! Identify any resistance you might have to receiving love and approval—from yourself or from others—and look for opportunities to give love and approval to yourself.

2. Explore ways to give love and approval to other people. The ways you show your love and approval can be subtle or more obvious, depending on what is appropriate for each person. You might greet a colleague warmly in the corridor, buy your partner a huge bunch of roses, or send a message of love and appreciation to someone through your thoughts or from your heart.

3. Accept people as they are—including yourself. Remember that acceptance is a pure form of giving love.

Exchanging Energy

We have looked at some of the more obvious ways in which people whisperers communicate, such as through words, the voice and body talk. Now let's move on to something which is a very exciting part of our relationships and which is everywhere in every moment: energy.

Energy flows in a huge number of ways between us and the other people in our world. It is exchanged in the words we use, our emotions, intentions, actions, through giving and receiving money, being in another person's space and through sex (oh yes!). Science is finally proving that everything in the universe is essentially pure energy: the stars, the planets, solid objects, thin air, you, me, everyone else and our emotions included. In fact, because everything in the universe is energy, there is just no getting away from it so we may as well flow with it.

People whisperers are always aware of the flow of energy between people and manage their own energy levels appropriately. They realize how essential it is to be vigilant during unhealthy exchanges of energy and take steps to protect themselves.

There are many different kinds of energy . . .

Energy can be explosive, creative, peaceful, loving and comforting, restorative, efficient, short-lived, steady and long-lasting, playful, heavy and serious, light and uplifting, quiet and secure, restless and unsettled . . . There are endless types of energy, but all basically emanating from the same raw material.

Any time we are with other people there is a flow of energy. Even when we are not actually in someone's vicinity, energy can still be flowing between ourselves and them. Sometimes there is a real surge of energy, sometimes a trickle. Sometimes the energy is mostly one-way, from one person to the other, and sometimes it flows back and forth between people in a more balanced way. Sometimes the flow of energy is healthy and sometimes it isn't.

Remember, as we saw in Secret Two, you do not have to be talking to someone or be within earshot of them to be communicating: you are still communicating on an energy level, whether you are audible or not.

Ask yourself:

✦ Do you have certain people in your life who leave you feeling drained and tired after you've been with them?

✦ Do you have other people in your life who leave you feeling buzzing, high or inspired?

Managing Energy

Before we start to manage the exchange of energy between ourselves and other people, it is a good idea to become aware of, and responsible for, our own levels of energy. Of course our energy levels go up and down at various times according to our biorhythms and whatever is going on around us. If we are involved in a dull task (sitting in boring school lessons comes to mind) our energy levels are liable to be down; if we are doing something exciting (like being out on an exciting first date) our energy levels will be up.

We all have natural energy levels that are characteristic of our personalities, which are fine, provided those levels do not cause difficulties when we interact with other people. For example, if you are a highly energetic person you may be too much for someone who is naturally quiet, and that may not help your relationship or communication. Equally, if you are low energy and you are trying to get a point across to someone high-energy, you may be best to increase your energy level to match your hyper companion for a while.

To manage your own energy levels in different situations is quite simple: but first you need to be "aware" of your energy levels. Becoming aware of your personal energy is simply a matter of taking the time to notice what is happening within you.

Ask yourself:

✦ What is my energy level like at the moment? For example, is it low, near death, high or explosively hyper, or calm and steady?

✦ In this moment, what would be the most beneficial energy level?

✦ When with another person ask: is my current level of energy an appropriate match for this person? If it is, great! If it is too high, "allow" the energy in your body and mind to lower; if it is too low, take in some energy-giving breath, think exciting thoughts and raise your levels.

Healthy Energy

A healthy exchange of energy between people is one where no one feels depleted as a result of being together. When participants all feel that they have been energized by being together then that is even healthier. For a healthy exchange of energies to take place each person has to accept the other, to validate their views and give them the space to be themselves. That doesn't mean you can't disagree, but ideally any disagreement will not carry a negative emotional charge with it, otherwise there may be a conflict, a winner and a loser. In effect, the winner draws energy from the loser and the loser suffers a loss of energy. (We will look at this in more detail in Secret Ten.)

Think about ways to bring positive energy flows
to personal and business relationships.

We get back whatever we give out: so if you help others to gain energy from being with you, without it depleting you, there will be all kinds of benefits for you in return.

If you help your partner to experience a flow of loving energy when you are together, they will be inclined to spend more time interacting with you rather than watching TV, being out with their friends or staying late at work. They will look forward to being with you, talking to you, being close and exchanging energies with you in many ways, not least making love and sharing tenderness and intimacy. If you deplete energy from your partner what might they do? Well, you may know that already.

If you are in business and every client you talk to feels uplifted by meeting you, they will probably want to see more of you. They will buy more of your products, buy you lunch, tell other people about you, give you energy in return and may even try to headhunt you for a more rewarding job with twice the money!

On the other hand, if you drain precious energy from your business clients, they will attempt to see you as little as possible. They will feel exhausted when they talk to you; restrict the amount of energy they send your way in the form of business and they may tell other people to avoid you or maybe not even mention you at all.

Unhealthy Energy

It is fine to exchange energy with another person if we agree to it, but it is not fine if that person begins to take energy from us without our "permission."

In an unhealthy exchange of energy, one person gains energy by affecting the emotional state of the other—by attempting to make them feel bad, frustrated, angry, confused, belittled, controlled or by dominating the situation using overt aggression or subversive, sneaky ways. By trying to make themselves look better than you or having a more valid and superior opinion, someone can draw energy off you and use it to build up their own energy level.

Sometimes people draw energy off another by using their intimate knowledge of that person. This is why it can be risky to get very close to another person: unless they are very delicate with you, they can easily draw energy off you by using that closeness to get under your armor.

Have you ever felt a time when someone used their closeness to you to gain emotional energy from you? Yes, I'm sure you have. Now here's another question for you: have you ever used your closeness to someone to gain emotional energy from them? Oooh. Yes, most of us have to admit to that at some time or another as well, I guess.

VAMPIRES AND TIDAL WAVES

Vampires

The myth of vampires may not be so far from the truth. There are people you meet in life who are so thirsty for energy that they will try to suck it right out of you, whether they are aware of it or not. Now I am not suggesting you hang garlic around your neck and carry a wooden stake in your hand, but it is useful to be aware of these kinds of exchanges. There are ways in which you can protect yourself from being "vampirized," but firstly you need to notice that it is happening—yes, it's our old friend "awareness" again. Someone can only take energy from you if you allow them to. If you choose not to allow it, you can protect yourself in a number of ways, e.g. by imagining you are surrounded by a force field that they cannot penetrate. You could also walk away from the situation, which is not always such a bad choice; if there was a real live vampire in front of you what would you do? Let's face it, you'd probably run like hell.

Tidal waves

Some people have so much energy that they flood and engulf others with it. It is marvelous that someone feels they want to burst their energy out all over you, but often they don't have any control over it and it chaotically gushes out everywhere. By sharing a load of excess energy with us, they may find some relief, but leave us feeling swamped.

> Being with someone who has far too much energy may be a bit like winning a million cans of beer: great in principle, but where are you going to put them all?!

Being with a tidal wave can be inspiring and exciting, but coping with someone who has a huge excess of energy can also use up a huge amount of our own energy and leave us feeling as drained as having been too near to a vampire. Energy is not something that can be stored or destroyed, so if someone dumps more energy on you than you can comfortably handle, you're going to have to find something to do with it all.

EXCHANGING ENERGY IN BALANCE

People whisperers only give as much energy as the person they are with can take and only receive the amount of energy that they in turn can handle.

Be aware that some people will need you to tone down your energy levels for them to be comfortable and others may need you to increase your energy levels for them to become engaged and involved in what you are doing.

Allowing Energy to Flow

It is natural for energy to flow constantly: the more you allow energy to flow through yourself and the people in your life, the more potential for joy is created. Look at the ways in which energy moves around the planet. Nature stores energy in relatively small amounts, such as the fat in an animal's skin for hibernation or nuts for squirrels to munch on, yet even in the earth's core energy is always circulating and occasionally bursts out at the surface. This is the natural way to use energy—allowing it to flow through your life, giving and receiving energy with other people, managing it in a balanced and sensible way so that it works for you and for the people in your life.

Use your energy to create the kind of relationships
and life you want.

Where you put your attention is where your energy will flow: if you put your attention on difficulties in your relationships and your life, that's what the energy will fuel; if your attention is on loving and positive connections, that is what the energy will fuel. Make it your mission to use your energy to create the kinds of relationships and life you want.

If you direct your energy in a very focused and clear way, you can use much, much less of it and still get the job done. Sometimes, using tiny amounts of focused energy can move mountains, whereas masses of unfocused energy would not have moved even a single stone.

Things to do:

1. Get into this "energy thing!" It is so interesting. Start to develop an awareness of your own energy levels at various times and in various situations.

2. Develop an awareness of when people are attempting to draw energy off you or when they are engulfing you like a tidal wave with too much energy. Take steps to be responsible for your own energy levels, without being tossed around by others.

3. Remember the universe is full of energy: if you need more energy, take a few moments to focus on your breathing and consciously breathe in some energy in the form of oxygen, allowing it to spread out through your body.

4. Avoid boosting your energy by simply borrowing it. Eating sugar and taking in caffeine are temporary ways to borrow energy. They give you a boost but you will have a lull again some time after.

CREATING RAPPORT

Rapport is a catalyst for cooperation; it is the knack of creating a connection between you and someone else that enables you to share common ground, be it in a conversation, through working together, loving each other, raising a family or creating some great works. Being good at creating rapport means knowing how to get on with people: empathizing, being authentic and honest, being happy about who you are and not judging who they are.

The Benefits of Creating Rapport

Having rapport with someone helps everything you do with that person to go more smoothly—more in the flow—and makes it possible to go further on the same amount of gas.

Although rapport is something that cannot be forced, theoretically it's possible to create rapport with anyone. That said, sometimes you may come across people who are resistant to rapport with you; if so, you have to decide at what point you stop investing energy in the relationship and accept you have done all you can, for now.

How to Create Rapport

To develop rapport you have to be true to yourself as much as possible: if you are not your true self it can be quite difficult for anyone to have rapport with you, as they won't know which of your "selves" to connect with.

In conversations, use the word "yes" more than the word "no"—such positivity is great for rapport.

An appropriate level of humor can also be helpful to loosen things up, but you need to be careful not to use humor at the expense of others, even someone who is not around. If you joke about someone not present, the person you're with could rightly assume that you might joke about them when they are not around.

To nurture rapport with someone, avoid attempts to come across as bigger, better or more impressive than you really are, or to dominate the conversation. These sorts of behavior tend to push people away rather than create rapport.

Things to do:

1. When you are with someone, even on first meeting, in what ways do you behave, speak or express yourself that may affect the other person?

2. Make a list of the people with whom you have good rapport. What are the benefits in your relationship of your rapport with each person? Now, think of some of the possible benefits that might come out of creating more rapport with people with whom you only have an acquaintance at present.

3. Watch the way people interact with each other and notice how they build or destroy rapport by the way they are. Think of some people who are good at creating rapport. How do they do it? What types of behavior make you feel comfortable with them; make you feel you could wear the same team shirt, that you share common views, that you could work or create something worthwhile together?

THE VALUE OF MEETING

Meeting people plays a large part in how we create opportunities for happiness, love, prosperity and success in our lives. The quality of our meetings dictates the level of possibility for happiness, love, prosperity and success. This is why skillful people whisperers appreciate the joys and the sense of possibility that meeting people creates: they endeavor to bring presence and value to every meeting and every person they meet.

The best kind of meeting is one in which everyone feels comfortable to be in each other's presence, and in which everyone has the opportunity to receive gifts in some way. It stands to reason that someone who is "well met" will be more inclined to give you whatever they can than someone who is "ill met." Helping other people to feel comfortable when you meet them is undoubtedly the best way forward, for you as well as for them.

First Impressions

Ask yourself:
- ✦ What kind of impression do you make when you first meet someone?
- ✦ What judgments, assessments and assumptions do you make about others from first impressions?

If you have any judgments, assumptions, preconceived or fixed ideas about people when you meet, you erect a barrier to the flow of possibilities. Even if you have met someone before, you cannot be sure that that person will behave in the same way as previously. They may have stuff going on in their lives we don't know about that drives their behavior, and it may not do so on the next occasion.

Creating the best impression doesn't mean pretending to be someone or something you are not. The way to give the best impression is to be true to yourself, while being aware of the other person's presence too. Think what impression your presence and body language give to people when they first meet you.

Ways to Create Positive Meetings

Create space: To create positive meetings with anyone, give the other person or people room in which to be themselves. Ask questions that help you to understand them and that allow them to enjoy sharing things about themselves with you.

Check your body's response: From time to time, remember Secret Three (Trust Your Body) and check your body internally. You want to feel peaceful and calm inside. Feel your body "open" to the other person, so you are sending out friendly energy alongside your verbal conversation. Remember that your external body also needs attention. Check what conversation your body is having with the other person's body, so you are sure your body is saying what you want it to say! Making your body appear passive and relaxed works best in most situations: have your eyes looking soft and present, look at the other person, but not in a staring or threatening way.

Handshakes: It is not so usual these days to shake hands during informal encounters in the Western world. Nevertheless, handshakes can be very interesting as there are so many things they can tell you about someone. A weedy handshake like a lettuce leaf might be saying "I'm timid," "I'm not really here" or "I'm not really interested in you." A strong handshake can be a way of trying to dominate and might be saying, "Feel how strong and tough I am, I can hurt your hand, even though my mouth is smiling." A very brief handshake might be saying, "I haven't got much time for you." A handshake where a finger secretly tickles your palm can mean either, "I'll meet you around the back of the bike sheds" or "Are you also a member of an ancient, secret, male-only society?"

Aim to leave everyone you meet happier
than they were before you arrived.

How to Prepare for Challenging Meetings

Sometimes we suspect that a meeting with someone is going to be challenging but we have to go ahead with it anyway, whether it is with our partner or spouse, the bank manager, a job interviewer, a blind date, our boss or our children's teacher! There are ways you can prepare for these encounters that will help you to stay balanced and even create successful relationships:

✦ Pay attention to your emotions as soon as they start to become unsettled, which may be just before you knock on the door, or it may be a day, a week or months before! However long it is before the meeting, when your emotions start to stir, practice allowing them to subside. Remember that stilling your emotions is easier when they are a gentle ripple, rather than when they are fully formed tidal waves. Being able to still your emotions will help you to avoid reacting or saying something inappropriate or impulsive in the meeting.

✦ Visualize having an invisible shield or defensive bubble around you to protect yourself from any harmful anger or attack. Although visualizing a shield may sound strange, it really works. There is no particular way that it has to be done: experiment to find a way that works for you personally.

✦ Use your physical body to still your emotions, which will also still your mind. Keep your attention focused on your lower stomach to help you stay centered and grounded. Feel *both* of your feet in contact with the ground and think of your feet as roots that anchor you down into the earth.

✦ Be still. Sit or stand in a way that is comfortable for you, so that you can be quite still during the meeting: this stillness gives a message of personal power to other people as well to yourself. Fiddling or continuing to adjust your body is an obvious sign of discomfort.

✦ Allow the other person or people to do most of the talking: remember that "a closed mouth gathers no feet!" Gather as few feet as possible by letting others express their stuff as much as you can. When you do speak, say exactly what you mean in a way that they will understand. Avoid speaking hurriedly. Listen to your tone of voice. Breathe in enough air before talking. Use phrases such as:

"I accept that is how it is for you."
"I guess we could agree to disagree."
"You have a point there: maybe you're right."
"This is how it is for me."
"I am sorry that you feel that way."

Things to do:

1. Enjoy all of your interactions and meetings with people. See every meeting as filled with potential: you never know who or where the next incredible phase of your life will come from.
2. Explore what happens for you emotionally, mentally and physically when you are with different people.
3. Remind yourself that most other people are at least as insecure in company as you, even if they appear to be self-confident.
4. Treat everyone in a way in which you would like to be treated by them.

BEING COMFORTABLE WITH STRANGERS

We have seen how the way we are when we meet people can profoundly influence our experiences and relationships. Now let's explore using people whisperer skills to create fulfilling relationships in the company of strangers.

Strangers present previously untapped possibilities for us, and it is often through our meetings with strangers that our lives are taken into new and exciting phases. We could be offering untapped possibilities for their lives, too. What happens when we put together two chemicals that have never been introduced before? Well, who knows—anything is possible! There could be a cataclysmic explosion, but equally there could be a discovery that sets humanity free from some of the bonds that tie it.

Being with people you have never met before can bring all manner of potential gifts; all you need to do is be there, stay open and nurture the situation. However comfortable or uncomfortable you may feel when you meet strangers, it is worth remembering that underneath, all people are human beings, and underneath that, we are all part of the same life force.

Ask yourself:

✦ When you meet strangers, do you ever feel uncomfortable or wonder what they think of you?

✦ Have you ever thought that they may be feeling uncomfortable and wondering what you think of them?

✦ Can you let go of your thinking, judging and forming of opinions about another person completely when you first meet them? How might that change the uncomfortable feelings you have?

We Are All One

When we don't know someone, it can be easy for us to imagine they are more accomplished in life: more successful, intelligent, powerful or generally more important than we are. But everyone comes into this world via the same basic route: a sperm and an egg get together, and the embryo grows in the womb and is born. The baby is helpless, cries, eats, cries, eats, vomits and fills diapers, grows up, lives however many years are allotted and then departs this world when the body gives out. This is the same for everyone.

Once we can be with people and recognize they are equal beings, we can take the invisible bond of equality that we share even further: we can meet them with love, knowing we are all a part of the same life force, part of the same creation, that they are us and we are them (as we will explore in Secret Twelve).

Shyness

Shyness is universally common, so once you realize that most people feel shy in some situations, it may not seem such a disadvantage. The truth is that what we focus on grows; so if we feel shy in certain company and start focusing on our shyness—which is what we usually do—it will increase! Instead of focusing on your shyness, it helps to focus on something else, such as the other person or people. If you stop thinking you should be a certain way and relax and be who you really are—self-contained and peaceful inside—the shyness will fade away.

Remember that some of the people who appear least shy are often the most shy. During my previous work as a musician and performer, I realized that one of the ways people cope with major shyness and insecurity is to hide it by becoming performers, thereby coming across as the total opposite of shy.

Things to do:

1. Next time you are going into a situation with strangers, remember that they may feel as insecure as you. Accepting that is the case, see what happens if you take steps to make them feel more at ease. Focus on the inner state of your body: simply be aware of what it is doing. This can have miraculous effects.

2. Practice being totally yourself: that means not pretending to be anything that you are not.

3. Give strangers the room to express themselves: encourage them to speak about themselves and what interests them. The more interesting you find them, the better it is for you.

4. Look for ways to meet more and more new people: they are part of the stream of humanity that brings newness into your life and will take you on to the next stage of your life.

We have discovered how giving love, exchanging energy and developing rapport are key ingredients for creating fulfilling relationships in all aspects of our lives—work and play. As you use these ingredients to enhance your bonds with others, it is important to remember that every person is a unique miracle, as we shall see in Secret Seven.

SECRET SEVEN
Get into Other People's Shoes

There have often been horse and rider combinations on my horsemanship workshops within which the owner is struggling with the horse's behavior. Recently a lady with a lovely appaloosa (the spotty horses originally bred by the Nez Perce Indians of North America) was moaning about how the horse bucked so much he was dangerous. She kept saying "He is such a pig, I hate him." She was right about the bucking: when asked to take up a right-lead canter the horse bucked like a bronco. She told me she had been trying to sort him and his problem out for a year or so and had even sent him away to a couple of well-known horse trainers in a bid to make him behave. But he still had the problem, or rather, she did!

Horses and people aren't stupid, they don't mess around without a reason, and my instincts told me the only way to resolve this was by asking the right questions. The questions I wanted to ask this little appaloosa were: what was making him buck? What was he experiencing that made him object to requests with such violence? Since he wasn't going to respond in words, I also needed to put myself in his shoes in order to investigate further. If I were wearing his shoes, what would I be thinking, feeling or believing that would make me buck like that?

I asked the lady to slow the horse down and alternate between walking and stopping. This was interesting, because if you looked carefully, each time he stopped his back legs stepped out a little to the left so that he stood crooked. I then asked her to get him stepping backwards and instead of walking backwards in a straight line he backed around to the left. It was becoming clear that this horse was uncomfortably stiff in one hind leg and was therefore protecting it. Anytime he was asked to do something which demanded strength in that leg, he was in pain. He communicated his pain almost constantly but wasn't being heard, so when it came to movements that really hurt his leg, such as a right-lead canter, he shouted in reaction to the pain in the only way he knew how: bucking. He was also expressing fear, because when he bucked he was being punished for it as disobedience, so now he was hurting *and* afraid.

I asked the horse to stand squarely on all four legs, stood behind him and was not surprised to see his hindquarters were a different shape on each side. The buttock muscles above the good leg were rounded and strong, yet the muscles above the stiff leg were atrophied, wasted and flat. I showed the owner. She didn't quite know what to think or feel when she realized her horse had been expressing pain and she had seen it as disobedience and begun hating him for it. She was at once embarrassed, relieved and guilty for how she had been treating him.

By stepping into this horse's shoes for a few moments it had become easy to understand why he had behaved as he did. We can also do this with people. It is perhaps all too often that we assume someone is being "difficult" when they are actually experiencing pain or fear, and by stepping into their shoes we gain an altogether different understanding.

The lady had her horse's physical weakness addressed with professional medical help and also undertook a suppling and strengthening training program. She also shifted her way of interpreting his behavior, stepping into his shoes and accepting he was communicating something she needed to hear. Both horse and owner are now building a better relationship together and getting along fine. Last time we spoke she said, "I love him to bits and would never part with him now."

People whisperers look at things from other people's points of view; they "walk in other people's shoes" in order to have more understanding, empathy and closeness with other people.

Wearing Another Person's Shoes

Have you ever wondered why someone does what they do, says what they say or believes what they believe? Slip into their shoes and you may begin to find out.

No matter how much time you spend with someone or how much you try to understand them, it will be impossible to ever really know what it is like to be another person. Every one of us has a unique set of experiences and we each have our own way of responding to all that happens to us. There are many examples of people who know someone really well and have been together in an intimate relationship for decades, and then suddenly their partner does something completely out of character and surprising.

We cannot be another person or ever fully know them, but what we can do is put ourselves in their position to give us more empathy and understanding of how things are for them. Wearing another person's shoes can be useful in so many situations: in a dispute with someone, making love with someone, wanting to motivate someone, wanting to sell something to someone or to nurture and help someone to learn.

Wearing another person's shoes can give you insight,
understanding, compassion, empathy and make you more loving.

Wearing another's shoes in a dispute

How many times have you found yourself digging into a position in an argument or disagreement? The other person digs into their position too, and the stage is set for you both to expend energy battling for your opinion as though your lives depended on it. You can change the whole dynamic for both of you if you wear their shoes for a moment. See things as they see them, feel what it feels like for them, hear what is being said through their ears.

Suddenly the dispute seems different. The more you ask them to describe how it is for them and understand their point of view, the easier it is to let go of the dispute. It doesn't mean that you agree with them or have to change your opinion, which you may end up doing, but by looking from the other person's angle, you begin to disentangle things, much like if you want to untie a knotted rope: you turn the knot around to see it from another angle to see where to start loosening it.

Wearing someone else's shoes in a dispute, especially with a loved one, takes great courage and awareness. It is even more difficult if you feel that you are being criticized or attacked for something. Often what sounds like personal criticism toward you isn't that at all, and once you are in the other's shoes you can begin to realize it is not personal.

Making love

Let's pick a nicer pair of shoes: how about making love? What is it like for the other person, the way you kiss them or the way you touch or stroke them? If you were them and feeling what they are feeling when you touch, kiss, stroke, tease, or join together, what would it be like? How would you want it to be? What ways might make it more pleasurable or interesting for them? As your hand touches their body, imagine it is touching your body. As your mouth kisses their mouth, imagine what that feels like to the person you are with.

Swapping shoes to gain support or motivation

If you want to gain someone's support or motivate them to your cause, it can be a great help to step into that person's shoes. What would make them really want to walk the extra mile for you? How do they view you in this situation? Do they think you have their interests at heart? By being in their shoes you see ways they can gain from the situation; you combine their agenda with your own and discover ways to gain their support and motivation.

Making a sale

If you want to sell something, it can be a great help to understand what makes your potential buyer tick. By stepping into their shoes you have a clearer understanding of what would make them think they needed your product. You also know more about how they are responding to your sales pitch and how you could pitch it differently to convince them to buy.

Smelly shoes!

The more you slip into another person's shoes and gain insight into how a person thinks, feels, sees and hears, the more empathy and understanding you will have. Even slipping into an unpleasant, smelly pair of shoes (metaphorically speaking) can help you to understand why someone is acting in an unacceptable, hurtful, boorish or antisocial way. That doesn't mean you agree with their behavior, but at least you understand more about what is driving it.

DEREK'S STORY

Derek enjoyed a high-level management position with an international bank. He was very successful in his work capacity and very effective at managing and leading the people in his team. But Derek was not so successful at relating to his teenage daughter and this was starting to make him feel uneasy even while he was at work, interfering with his concentration, eroding his self-confidence and making him feel edgy for much of his time in the office. In fact, the situation had become so bad that Derek and his daughter didn't communicate directly at all: their communications all took place via his wife.

When Derek talked about the situation during a workshop with me, he was clearly upset, but more than that—the more he talked about it, the more I could see how much brooding anger he had. One of the issues that he talked about the most was the disgusting, messy state of his daughter's room, which drove him mad. I asked Derek how he thought his daughter might feel about their relationship and how she might perceive him and the way he acted when she was around him.

He looked almost shocked by the question: he really hadn't thought how it might be for her or what she might think of the way he treated her. His response was something like, "Well, maybe she feels unloved and unwanted by me and thinks I don't even like her. I guess she sees the way I am as being bossy and angry with her all the time . . . hey, that would explain a lot!"

I asked how he might alter to help her feel different about him and his answer was very simple, "Well, I could see things from her point of view and let her be how she wants to be. Maybe stop being 'Mr. Angry' I suppose, and—if she wants to live in a room that's a mess—that's up to her, I don't have to live in it!"

I didn't even need to hear whether Derek's relationship with his daughter had improved after that session: there was such a profound change in his face, body language, energy and emotion in the instant when he put himself in her shoes that it was very moving for everyone present. There was no doubt that the father/daughter relationship had changed from that moment on, before they were even together again in the same room.

A Third Position: Wearing a "Fly on the Wall's" Shoes (Don't Say Yuk!)

Normally we wear our own shoes. If we think about it, we can attempt to wear other people's shoes. A third position we can take is that of an outside observer, like a fly on the wall. This gives us another angle to view things from and is the most objective position to be in. I am not suggesting you buzz around the light fitting and take an unhealthy interest in waste products left on the pavement by dogs; the fly on the wall is like an observer looking in, without taking any part in the proceedings aside from watching. This is a way to see what is happening between yourself and other people, without taking either side.

Of course it would a miracle if you could look at things totally objectively: everything you think, say and do is the product of years of conditioning, but being willing to look at something from the outside still gives you a fresh view, another angle from which to look at the same diamond, if you like.

The advantage of taking the third position is that it can loosen up your thinking and allow you to create new solutions. It can help you to let go of thoughts you are attached to and move you forward.

Positive Intentions

It may be hard to believe sometimes but, from their point of view, everything that anyone says or does is motivated in some way by a positive intention. However misguided their motivation for doing something might appear, somewhere deep in the recesses of their brain is a good reason for doing what they are doing. Of course, it may not seem like a good reason to you at all, but to them it is a beneficial reason to be doing or saying what they are doing or saying.

If you can wear another's shoes and see what their reason or positive intention is for their behavior, you will have taken a huge leap forward for man and mankind. Once you realize what is making someone do what they do, and see that they believe it to be positive in some way, the easier it is to deal with the situation.

It is important to realize that people's positive intentions are unconscious most of the time: they are motivated by the intention but aren't necessarily aware of it.

Certain behavior can be easy to understand, such as a when a baby (or an adult!) yells and throws their toys out of the stroller: the positive intention may be that they want more attention and love.

Sometimes it is slightly more difficult to discover the positive intention, e.g. when someone makes a cutting remark that makes you appear small, their positive intention may be to make themselves feel more important, significant and lovable in relation to others.

Some behavior is very difficult to understand in terms of positive intention, e.g. becoming a sadistic tyrant and convincing the population to turn into genocidal maniacs against the people of their neighboring countries. People who have done this will have had a positive intention hidden in there somewhere, albeit tough to understand and hard to believe.

Things to do:

1. Practice wearing someone else's shoes in a situation such as a dispute, especially where you are really adamant about your view being right.

2. Look for the possible positive intention behind what people say or do.

3. Practice being a fly on the wall and looking in at yourself and someone else while you interact with them.

4. Put yourself in another position when you are being intimate, kissing or making love: give yourself physically to the other person in a way that works for them by sensing it from their point of view. Give as you would receive.

5. Put yourself in the other person's shoes when you want them to buy into an idea or commit to something: if you can find out what they want and combine it with what you want, you will be blessed with great success.

Every Person Is Different

Every single person is different—that much is obvious. Yet, how often do we resist the fact that someone else thinks, behaves, talks or believes something differently to ourselves? We may think we are always accepted exactly as we are, and we accept other people as they are, but if we look deeper, we soon realize it is almost universal for people to have reservations, annoyances, doubts or judgments around others.

There really is great power in totally accepting someone for their own uniqueness: because when we truly accept other people, the whole communication process becomes wide open. Once the communication process is open anything is possible, because space has been created. This means there is no resistance and everything is free to flow in our interactions with others; all things become possible. People whisperers recognize, accept and delight in the uniqueness of every single person on the planet, which means they notice people's characteristics and keep them in mind when they communicate.

In a loving relationship, totally accepting the other person means infinite love, tenderness and intimacy can flow. In a work situation, total acceptance of someone enables all manner of business opportunities, possibilities and creativity to manifest themselves.

Accepting Ourselves As Different

Accepting others as different begins with accepting that you yourself are different. This can be a challenging thing to do, because from birth onward we are programmed to conform. From an early age we are made to feel uncomfortable in many situations for expressing our uniqueness. Particularly in situations such as those at school, we may try hard to fit in with the "in crowd" and avoid being on the outside of the gang. When we conform to the gang we squash our individuality. We do this to ourselves and we attempt to do it to others too: at school, anyone standing out from the crowd is a prime target for harassment and bullying, because they are daring to express their "difference."

The great achievers in life are often those who do the things that others say are impossible, and in so doing they dare to express themselves, their uniqueness and difference.

In adult life we still come under pressure to not express our uniqueness. In the workplace we become subject to the company culture: we toe the line, don't make waves or rock the boat. Companies need rogue monkeys and original thinkers, but their presence is often discouraged and, in some cases, feared.

Ask yourself:

✦ If you could express your uniqueness in any and every way you wanted, how would you be different to how you are now?

✦ What would you wear?

✦ What would you say to people?

✦ What would you do with your time?

Celebrating uniqueness in other people

When you accept someone is different, you approach them with an openness that means you notice more about that person. As a result of noticing more about someone you begin to communicate with them in a way that works better for them and, as a result, better for you too.

Think about someone with whom you have an intimate relationship or someone at work and think about ways they are different to you that you find challenging to accept . . . if they didn't have those aspects to their character, surely they wouldn't be who they are today? Their uniqueness is one of the reasons you have attracted them into your life and if it is something challenging for you to accept, they have come into your life with a gift for you: the gift is perhaps the opportunity for you to expand and learn from them. Once you can fully accept someone you find challenging as different in all of their ways, they will either miraculously change, pass peacefully out of your life or you will become far more intimate and close to them. Either way, accepting someone is different means you cannot lose!

Learning from Others

The uniqueness of everyone in your life is a vast source of information for you. By watching the people in your life behaving in ways that are different to you, you can see them do things which work and things that really don't work!

When you see people doing things that work well, you can experiment by copying what they do to see if it works for you too. Likewise, when you see people doing things that make it harder for them, you can avoid making some of the same mistakes.

Things to do:

1. Celebrate your own individuality. Follow it by celebrating other people's originality: find other people fascinating, amusing, impressive, sad, inspiring, unfathomable, unbelievable, incredible and lovable. Once you start looking, you will be amazed!

2. Think of a few ways in which you are totally unique and different from anyone else you know. If you can't think of anything, start exploring how you might be if you were free to be or do things exactly as you wanted: how would you be different from others if you allowed yourself to be?

3. Think of someone who does something that you find annoying or challenging: see if you feel different about it if you change the way you view their behavior. Instead of seeing it as annoying, re-label it by recognizing it as simply them "expressing their uniqueness."

4. Start looking at everyone you come into contact with and see-ing how they express themselves by the clothes they choose to wear. Even when they dress to look similar to others there are still little badges of uniqueness, e.g. jewelry, hairstyle, shoes, or the way they present "themselves" to the world.

5. Take a trip around a housing estate of uniformly built houses: notice how, despite every house being built the same, the inhab-itants have displayed endless imagination in making their house represent something of their uniqueness and identity, whether it is done by neglect, an amusing array of gnomes or by adding stone cladding, grand entrance gates, a portcullis and battlements!

Stepping into other people's shoes will help you to see the world from their perspective, but it is equally important to respect the boundaries between you. At times it may seem that your differ-ences are insurmountable or that conflict is inevitable. On these occasions people whisperers deploy the skills described in Secret Eight.

SECRET EIGHT
Have Healthy Boundaries

It was a typical stormy English fall morning on Exmoor—driving rain coming in sideways and the wind whipping in from the southwest. To rescue the horses from being exposed to any more of the foul weather, a number of us were leading two horses each down the stony track and into the shelter of the farmyard. The horses were highly excited, agitated and skittish because of the wild rain and wind.

Unbeknown to the horses, someone had innocently left a board of plywood on the grass verge by the side of the lane: horses notice everything and are highly suspicious of anything new. The horses I was leading leapt sideways away from the board as we passed it. I looked back to see the girl following me with her two horses arriving at the board of wood, at which point, both horses lunged forward into the back of her, knocking her to the ground as though she were invisible. I watched in horror as the two horses ran over her body for what seemed like an eternity. She was rolled down the rain-drenched stone track like a rag doll being trampled repeatedly by eight iron-shod feet, as the horses desperately tried to escape from the object of their fear, her body under their feet. To add to their panic, they imagined that she was trying to grab hold of their legs, and this made matters worse.

After the horses had disappeared, she lay still for a few moments and then, by some miracle, found that she could sit up. But as she looked over at me I could see a hole the size of a large coin in the center of her forehead and the rather sickening sight of yellowy-white bone of her skull showing.

This was a powerful lesson for me in setting boundaries. Horses weigh around half a ton each and are hugely stronger and faster than a human. For that reason I have a boundary which I hold to this day under any circumstances with horses: they must stay out of my body space. This is a non-negotiable boundary. In fact this boundary makes things easier for the horses, because there is no question about it, no inconstancy, and no time when I blur the edges: they know that this boundary exists and that helps them to know how to be with me. If the two horses in the incident had stayed out of the girl's body space they would have avoided her rather than knocking her to the ground.

The girl in the accident had stitches to her forehead and was the proud owner of horse-shoe shaped bruises from head to toe, but after a few weeks of rest and recovery, she was scarred but otherwise fine.

When I go out into the fields to see my horses they usually come over to see me and we play and run together. Without my non-negotiable boundary in place, running free with a bunch of playful loose horses could be dangerous. In fact there are occasions when it is not appropriate for me to be playing so closely with my horses; if they are too high on energy, if they want to push me around or get into a conflict with me, I will clearly and lovingly send them away from me across the paddock to behave in that way elsewhere.

How simple would it be if we established and maintained boundaries as clearly as that with people, if we dealt with conflict and calmly put a distance between us and other people when they behave in ways that are not OK for us? Horses can do us a lot of harm, but people can hurt us deeply in so many ways too.

EXPLORING "BOUNDARIES"

People whisperers know that to create loving relationships based on trust and respect they need to have healthy boundaries. They also accept and abide by the boundaries that other people put in place.

Boundaries are like lines drawn between what is acceptable to us physically, mentally and emotionally, and what is not acceptable. They are not barricades or walls, but represent a reasonable way of saying to others that "This is what is acceptable to me" and "that is not."

Think of a boundary as a permeable membrane (you remember biology lessons at school). Boundaries work like filters; they stop unwanted behavior from passing through, while allowing acceptable behaviors through to us from others. E.g. they may filter out someone's unreasonably angry communications to us, but allow their loving communications through.

Boundaries and Love

When you establish boundaries it doesn't mean that you are not being loving; you can still be very loving, but you are also helping someone to see what sort of behavior is OK for you and what would be going too far. Boundaries are a kind way of guiding someone to behave in a way that is acceptable when that person is around us. Boundaries help others to know where they stand, and then respect and closeness can follow.

In intimate relationships, where there is closeness and deep knowledge of the other person, it is very common for boundaries to be violated (although that sounds like a strong word).

Boundary-less relationships are usually more dysfunctional than those in which both partners know where they stand.

Boundaries can be a very tricky area for people and are often disrespected in various aspects of our lives. Boundaries can be about behavior, sense of personal space, finances, use of time, sexual behavior, drinking or things that are said. They may be about how you express love and how much work or what type of work is acceptable to you. They may be quite specific, such as what time your teenage son has to be home at night and how loudly he can play his horrendous music, or whether your boss can call you at home on a Sunday morning.

Meeting Resistance to Boundaries

Some people will test your boundaries quite determinedly. In these cases you have to hold fast, control your emotions and know where you have drawn the line on what is acceptable. Once the pressure is off, you can always review your boundaries and consider whether or not they are still appropriate or necessary. If you allow someone to destroy your boundaries, the resulting ill feeling will not help you or the other person. . . unless it teaches you to hold fast next time.

People who refuse to accept your boundaries are saying something to you about how they don't respect you as an individual. With some people you may need to mark out your boundaries in a particularly clear, emphatic way. To do this without bringing negative emotions up from inside you when setting or reaffirming your boundaries can be very challenging.

It is normal to set different boundaries with different people in your life: if you set the same boundaries with your work colleagues as you do with your loving partner, the workplace could soon become a very confused place!

When you set new boundaries, people who are not accustomed to them may react in ways that can be difficult and uncomfortable for you. They may try to make you alter or erase your new boundaries using any approach they can, ranging from anger and intimidation to increased tenderness and softly-softly methods. This is usually a temporary phase but it does need you to be strong and lovingly stick to those new boundaries.

Boundaries Are Our Human Right

Certain people in your life, such as those who are dominant or vulnerable, or those with whom you have close intimacy, may make it quite difficult for you to believe that you are allowed to set boundaries or to say "no" to something. Peer pressure is a very common way for people to transgress your boundaries: everyone will be familiar with jibes such as "Go on, have another drink, you lightweight," or "Everyone else will be going, you've got to come, what's wrong with you?"

Everyone sets boundaries at their own level: some people can tolerate being more encroached upon by others or put up with less decorous behavior than other people can. People whose boundaries have been disrespected many times may react by erecting impenetrable boundaries for themselves, as a means of defense against future attack. These people can experience serious emotional and mental problems as a result of the lack of respect that has been shown to them and their boundaries in the past.

If someone is pushing against your boundaries, that person is confirming that you still need the boundaries in place.

Being Consistent

One of the keys to maintaining boundaries successfully is communicating them to other people in a way that they understand. It is no good setting boundaries, keeping them to yourself and then slicing someone's head off when they overstep the mark— the poor now-headless person didn't know the boundary was there until it was too late.

It is essential to be as consistent as possible if your boundaries are to work: if you chop and change your boundaries with someone, that person will not know where they stand and become either very nervous or disrespectful around you.

Although you need to be consistent for your boundaries to work, it doesn't mean they are written in stone and cannot be altered when your relationships or circumstances change. Boundaries need to play a natural and healthy part in everyday life, and not be ignored or over-emphasized . . .

Balance is a key word with boundaries, and having boundaries can help to maintain balance in our lives.

Remember that boundaries are not only about your interactions with other people: you have to set boundaries for yourself too, about such things as how you behave, how you manage your appetites for fun, food, drink or sex, how much work you do and how much money you spend.

DAVID AND JAN'S STORY

David and Jan were brother and sister. In many ways they had always been very close. Unfortunately, their closeness seemed to make David think he could say whatever he liked to Jan and she would just take it, which she always had—for the first sixty-three years of their lives together anyway! Clearly David and Jan had no idea about the need for establishing respectful boundaries between them. They probably hadn't needed boundaries as small children growing up so closely together, but now as adults in their sixties, they were in danger of losing each other for good.

When Jan spoke to me, she was upset about some very personal comments David had made to her about her husband and one of their daughters. Jan and her family had been invited to spend Christmas with David's family, but because of what had been said, she did not want to go. Yet felt she couldn't say "no" for fear of offending him or because he might "lay into her" if she explained how she felt. Her only solution, as she saw it, was to duck out altogether and not get in touch with him at all, hoping the whole thing would blow over, somewhat like an ostrich burying its head in the sand.

I asked her to think about what she wanted to do about Christmas and what would be most comfortable for her. She said she didn't feel she wanted to visit David, so I suggested that she call him and decline the invitation, but also let David know she was hurt by what he had said, in a totally calm and emotionally uninvolved way. To achieve this, I suggested she wait however long it took until her body felt still inside, and while she made the phone call, she focused constantly on the inner stillness in her body. I suggested that when she spoke to her brother she calmly say what she wanted to say and then tell him that she did not feel it was appropriate to discuss it any further with him at that time.

Jan took a few deep breaths and made the call in my presence. She was calm, focused, unemotional and clear; she laid out the facts and avoided apportioning blame: she was brilliant. Jan had set her first healthy boundary with her brother after sixty-three years of feeling like his much-loved punching bag. What a relief! David's reaction was one of regret, surprise, apologies and a few tears: he had probably never realized how his unbridled comments had hurt the sister he loved so much. David went quiet for a couple of weeks after her call while he regained his equilibrium, but Jan held her nerve and finally they began communicating again, now with the respect and adult boundaries in place that Jan deserved.

Things to do:

1. Start thinking about boundaries you have in place with the people you love. Do those boundaries work, or do you need to change or reinforce them? Experiment with putting a couple of new boundaries in place about relatively minor things, such as who makes the coffee in the morning.

2. Explore what boundaries you may need to set for yourself. Consider those areas in which you have the fewest boundaries and ask yourself what underlying needs are being met by your allowing those areas to run amok. For example, overeating may be a way of meeting the need to feel more loved. Indulging a rampant sexual appetite could be a way of meeting the need to feel more loved. Or, spending too much money visiting the mall for a bit of retail therapy could be a way of meeting the need to—you guessed it—feel more loved . . . Is there a pattern emerging here?!

3. Begin to put small boundaries in place if you need to. But be aware that if you are not used to setting boundaries, it may be challenging at first to do this without getting emotionally involved. For example, you may feel slightly aggressive or edgy about it.

Personal Space

Having healthy boundaries includes the need to understand personal space. Personal space is an interesting thing: have you ever been on a crowded beach in summer looking for a patch of sand on which to set up "camp"? Think about the way the people on the beach have spread themselves out and how they set up those temporary territorial areas. What makes you walk along the beach carrying your picnic, blankets, sunscreen, beachball, surfboard, etc., and reject certain spots? Then finally . . . what makes you pick a particular spot?

It is a similar phenomenon whenever you walk down a crowded shopping street. Isn't it amazing how rarely anyone bumps into anyone else? And when someone does bump into you and breaks that unwritten law of crowded shopping malls "thou shalt not bump into anyone," you feel affronted and give them a grumpy look, or apologize immediately. Somehow we can all tell intuitively how much personal space is right for us.

People whisperers are aware of their own personal space and are equally aware of the personal space belonging to other people; they show respect by being an appropriate and comfortable distance for each situation and each individual person.

Your Personal Space

What does your personal space mean to you? Perhaps it is a safety zone around you or an invisible skin. Clearly, society has a generally agreed guide to personal space, but within those guidelines, everyone has their own feelings about how much personal space they need to be comfortable.

Depending on the kind of person you are with, the sense of how much personal space you need changes. With some people it can feel wonderful to allow them close into your personal space. If you both feel comfortable, this can be a subtle way of exchanging energy and love.

By reading the signals given off by people's body language and attitude, including strangers, normally we know what distance needs to be kept between us. Unfortunately, some of the most uncomfortable train, plane and bus journeys can be the result of having to be nearer to a certain person's personal space than you feel is right!

MY STORY

I was unfortunate enough to have a driving instructor who liked to sit with his arms across the back of both seats and move his face in really close to me to talk while I drove. This was very uncomfortable, as it was high summer and the poor guy had rather noticeable B.O. and halitosis too. I learned to drive with my head out of the window, and it sure was an incentive to pass my driving test first time!

Using Body Space

You can use your awareness of personal space and where you place your body relative to other people as a way of communicating with them. For example, standing well back from someone could be telling them that you are unsure or are waiting to know them better before "getting close." Some people may invade your personal space in order to appear intimidating or dominating, almost as though they are threatening to take up your space in the world. Paradoxically, standing close in someone's body space can be a way of sharing intimacy and warmth with someone: it all depends on how it is done and with whom!

The angle of your body also has an effect on what you communicate to others. If you stand facing head-on to someone, you are interested and fully engaging with that person. Standing head-on can also be used as a dominant position. If you stand with your body at a slight angle away from the person you are with, they may feel more comfortable, but they may think they don't have your full attention.

Things to do:

1. Become aware of what distances feel comfortable when you talk to different people. Look for the subliminal signals that tell you to be nearer or further away from others.

2. See how people position themselves in relation to you. Next time you stand in a line, notice how you can feel the presence of the other people in it and whether it is uncomfortable when they stand too close to you.

3. Be aware of when someone takes up your body space to be dominant or intimidating. Once you realize they are doing this, it no longer has power over you; it may just make you chuckle!

Who Is in Control Here?

Having good boundaries and a respect for personal space are important ingredients in healthy relationships, but as we have seen, these are also areas where people attempt to control and dominate each other. Pecking orders exist naturally within many animal species and the human race is no exception; unfortunately, there are areas of human interaction in which control and dominance are unhealthy and unwelcome.

People whisperers notice unnecessary control, dominance or subservience patterns when they happen and avoid engaging in them: instead they choose to maintain boundaries and approach every person as an equal divine being.

Dominance and Insecurity

The most controlling and dominating people in the world are often the most insecure. If someone is attempting to control or dominate you, by understanding their behavior you will realize that they are probably being driven by fear and inadequacy. Their behavior may be an attempt to make up for aspects of their character in which they experience fear, lack or self-doubt.

Our fearful human ego often makes us want to control people and events in order to make life seem safe and more comfortable, and to save ourselves from largely imagined pain or death. These driving factors of the ego are largely unconscious in people but they can have a very powerful influence on behavior.

> Our fearful ego makes us believe that if only we can control events, and more particularly other people, we will be safe. But this is an illusion of global proportions.

Control and dominance at home

Practically all people play controlling, dominating, subservient or submissive games in some area of their lives, if not in most areas. In many intimate relationships when two people live closely together, it is "normal" for control and dominance games to be played out. One partner may use their intimidating tone to get their own way; another may use the withdrawal of affection, intimacy or sex to gain their agenda; and yet another may play a weak, helpless victim role to gain control of their partner. Control can be a very slippery issue and in relationships it may be the person who appears to be outwardly submissive who is really the dominant partner, since that person may be using subtle means to manipulate their partner.

Control and dominance at work

Many kinds of dominance and control situations are found in the workplace. Your job position dictates to some degree your status in relation to the people "above" and "below" you. Being in a position of authority does not mean there is a need to control or dominate: it is possible to be a very successful leader of people without resorting to patterns of unhealthy control or domination. Being a leader without waving the big stick of command and control is a hot subject in today's corporations, because it is quite a nebulous skill to define, whereas waving a big stick is fairly easy to define!

One way to tell the difference between true leaders and bad leaders lies in the comments made by their followers. People find true leaders inspiring and motivating, encouraging them to do the best they can. Poor leaders don't generate the same enthusiasm. Which would you rather work for?

Being a successful leader or person in authority
does not require you to be controlling or dominant.

There are people who find it difficult to handle their authority over others. To avoid jeopardizing their popularity or relationships with their staff, some people do not take up the leadership role that they are meant to play, choosing instead to be ineffective. Being ineffective is not the opposite of dominance and control, and being a leader or person in a position of authority does not necessarily mean that you are controlling. Do not shy away from using your authority as and when necessary for fear of being disliked, otherwise you are the one being controlled!

Predators and Prey

There are people who feel the need to go through life acting like predators most of the time: they do this to get their own way and dominate others. Of course, predators can only be successful if someone else is willing to act like prey.

Predator People are normally aggressive, over-powering, armed with teeth and claw (yes, I had a schoolteacher just like that), hungry and self-interested. The positive side of predator profiles is that they get things done, they take risks, they are bold, they are tenacious and go-getters.

Prey People are timid and fearful. They get pushed around, they lack ambition and drive and are constantly looking for a peaceful time where they can get on with life without being eaten! The positive side of prey profiles is that they get along with others easily, they don't rock the boat, they are steady, consistent and won't kill you!

Which role do you slip into most, predator or prey?
In what situations do you find yourself acting like a predator?
In what situations do you find yourself acting like prey?

Things to do:

1. Explore areas of your relationships where you find yourself acting in a dominant and controlling way; not just in obvious predator-like ways, but in sneaky subtle ways too. Ask yourself what you might be afraid of or insecure about that gives you the need to act in this way.

2. Look at any of your relationships where you allow others to dominate or control you. The ways this can happen may be very subtle: you will have to be very vigilant. For each person, list three simple steps you could take to redress the balance.

3. Remember, someone can only really dominate you if you allow them to: even if they can *make* you do something, they cannot dominate your inner space if you don't give them permission. Practice becoming transparent in situations where you may be dominated, rather than confronting the dominator.

4. For a brief period, let go of control in an area of your life where you are normally quite controlling. This could be at home, in the bedroom, at a community group, or at work. See how it feels to let go of control; see where it takes you.

5. If you are in a position of authority, experiment with the ways in which you could express your power positively. Remember that your inner state is what primarily affects other people: be sure not to load your authority with a negative emotional charge.

Conflict

Despite having respectful boundaries and being aware of control and dominance, people whisperers know conflict is a natural part of life. They don't withdraw from conflict when it is unavoidable, but do what they can to minimize the damage caused to themselves, other people and the universe. You would be very rare if you could live your whole life without experiencing some kind of conflict at some point. Even "enlightened" people are likely to experience times of conflict in their lives.

What Do We Mean by Conflict?

Conflict is what happens when people have opposing views, with each side making a stand for what they believe is right. Conflict is a natural part of life: birds do it, dogs do it, horses do it, people do it and even educated fleas do it! It is natural for us to have different viewpoints and agendas to other people from time to time: no matter how impeccable you are, there is always the chance that someone will manage to fall out with you over something at some time in your life.

Conflict is not the problem,
it is how you handle it that matters.

Conflict can be an internal experience as well as an external one; you can be at loggerheads with yourself over an issue as much as you can be in disagreement with another person or people.

The benefits of conflict

Since conflict appears to be natural, we can assume that it has some gift or value to it. Conflict that is healthily expressed can clear the air, release tension and offer a way to move forward. It can stretch us to find new resources and can be a place from which to build something stronger, including a stronger relationship. A tree that is battered by the wind will have stronger roots and branches as a result. (Too much battering will stunt its growth and blow the fruit to the ground before it is ripe, however.)

Because conflict is usually uncomfortable, it can push us to learn and grow.

Many of the most rapid and helpful discoveries and advances in science have occurred as a result of international conflict. On a personal level, when we are stretched by conflict we may find extra resources, new strengths and skills within ourselves.

Conflict in an intimate relationship can be a very positive sign: at least the other person feels comfortable, safe and empowered enough within the relationship with you to express themselves freely!

The downsides of conflict

Although it is possible to view conflict as serving some positive purposes, it can easily become destructive and unpleasant if it is not handled with care, respect and delicacy. Conflict uses valuable energy and can cause separation between people. It can be unloving and harmful, breeding distrust and hate, and causing lasting damage.

Options

Since conflict is a part of human life, you may need various options in order to deal with it.

1. You can simply avoid it or withdraw from it. (Unfortunately, avoiding or withdrawing from conflict can limit your progress through life and it usually has a way of catching up with you somewhere along the line.)
2. You can let it permanently affect you (which is not ideal).
3. Or finally, you can learn to handle conflict with skill and courage, as you would handle any potentially dangerous animal . . . "Yes, now that sounds interesting!"

> Remember that most people are very sensitive and easily hurt. Like a wounded animal, a person that is hurt is less easy to reason with.

21 Ideas for Handling Conflict

1. State your point of view as clearly as possible but keep your emotions out of it: don't be overtaken by anger, etc. Notice your emotions and be aware of them.
2. Look for ways to go through the process and resolve it with the minimum damage caused to yourself, your opponents and to the environment.

3. Be aware of your strong attachment to needing to be right. It may be there is no right or wrong in the situation; in fact, all sides may be in the right, depending on your viewpoint. Ask yourself: how can I be different in this situation that might help toward resolution?

4. Stick to dealing with the present and avoid dragging up the past.

5. Look for a way forward, rather than going round in circles.

6. Remain as quiet and still inside and out as you can.

7. Step into the other person's shoes. See what gives them the opinions, feelings or viewpoints they have. Step out of both your own and the other person's shoes and be an intelligent fly on the wall: what is it like listening in from outside of the conflict?

8. Silently project a sense of unconditional love toward your "opponent" through the crossfire. Experience how this changes the dynamic, especially if there is a lot of hate and anger in the air.

9. Avoid making personal or insulting comments.

10. You may need to "agree to disagree." This is probably the most sensible solution in the majority of cases. The truth is, both sides will have a point of view they believe in; otherwise they wouldn't be in conflict. Accept that you both see things differently.

11. Avoid scoring points. Conflict is too costly to be a sport; it can cost more than money can buy.

12. See what happens if you simply say, "Well, you may be right." Now, that could be a very brave step!

13. Dealing with challenging people may require you to give them time to find their balance: challenging people often bring great rewards and gifts with them, if you have the strength, love and patience to handle them.

14. Be sure you understand exactly what your opponents mean and they understand exactly what you mean. A great deal of conflict is unnecessarily caused by poor communication or lack of understanding of each other's message.

15. Know that however insane someone's action or belief, there is always a "positive intention" behind it (see Secret Seven). Ask yourself "What is the positive intention behind them taking this stand?"
16. Remember there is no shame in walking away from a conflict in which the opponent is superior to you and may inflict too much damage upon you.
17. There is no honor in fighting "to the death" unnecessarily with someone over an issue. Be noble and find a solution that doesn't involve creating an outright victor, otherwise you may have created animosity that will return to haunt you one day.
18. Make it an important goal to preserve the relationship and keep goodwill with the other side: if you find an outcome in which you have preserved or even strengthened the relationship, then both sides are winners.
19. If you don't feel emotionally capable of dealing with something right away, be fair to the other person by giving them a commitment to talk again at a certain time on a certain day. Otherwise you are leaving them "hanging."
20. When you are speaking to someone to resolve conflict, speak from your heart: don't plan what you're going to say in your head too much, but allow the words you need to come "through" you. Let yourself be guided and be in the flow.
21. Healing rifts between people is like healing a wound: it can take time and care, which means handling the wound with delicacy until it is stronger and avoiding stressing it with emotions such as impatience or anger.

Things to do:

1. Accept that conflict is a part of life. Do all that is possible to avert outright conflict, but be careful not to become a conflict avoider as this is not an honest way to have relationships (I know, because I've done it!).
2. Look for the gift in any conflict and you will change the dynamic of the situation.

3. Watch how people run their conflicts: become interested in people's "conflict style" and then study your own conflict style. Ask yourself how you could alter your approach in conflict so that it is less painful and bloody, and more productive for you and your opponents.

4. Let me wish you luck!

Whose "Stuff" Is It Anyway?

Conflict arises and healthy boundaries become blurred when people's "stuff" comes up. What often happens when two or more people come together is the baggage they each bring with them is brought to the surface.

What we are talking about here is emotional baggage: junk that gets in the way, personal hang-ups and issues, patterns that cause difficulty, limiting beliefs etc. It is not necessarily easy for us to see what stuff we have, let alone admit to ourselves that it is in there. People whisperers are aware of the need to recognize who is bringing stuff into a conversation or relationship and they attempt to take responsibility for their own baggage.

We may live reasonably easily with our own baggage so long as we are not involved with anyone else, but when someone else turns up, and most especially in close personal relationships, our stuff surfaces and difficulties arise. What also happens when two or more people get together is that their stuff becomes entangled and confused: it can be hard to know whose stuff is whose, since what we unconsciously do is attempt to pin our stuff on the other person by all kinds of subtle means. This entanglement can cause quite a lot of upset between people, as this unconscious game of denying or pretending our stuff is someone else's is played out, in the hope that we won't be found out and have to take responsibility for it! People whisperers recognize other people's baggage and choose to handle it with sensitivity, rather than being burdened by it.

So the question is this: "Whose stuff is it anyway?"

And another question has to be: "What is my stuff and where did I get it from?"

You may also wonder: "How do I take responsibility for my stuff and not for anyone else's?"

Emotional and Mental Toxins

Just as having a body full of toxins would inhibit our physical performance, so the build-up of emotional and mental "stuff" inhibits our free-flowing experience of life. Sometimes we can be virtually crippled into inaction by the build-up of emotional and mental toxins formed since we were in the womb. Recognizing that we suffer from emotional and mental toxins, and that they prevent us from realizing our full potential, is the first step to becoming free of them. We may have carried some stuff in our system for so long that we cling to it and believe it is "just how we are" or "who we are," or an integral part of.

If you feel any emotions rise or feelings stir in your body, you know that you are bringing your own stuff to the situation in which you find yourself. And once you know what stuff is yours, you can begin to see what stuff doesn't belong to you. If you feel "wobbly" in a particular situation, you can ask yourself whose stuff it is: yours or someone else's? The chances are it may be both! It is also worth recognizing that if someone is being overly critical they are usually being motivated by their own stuff. Mind you, if you are bothered by them being critical, that is your stuff! It can take a great deal of honesty and courage to admit it is your stuff in the context of a relationship, as blaming another person often seems far easier!

What Is "Running" You?

We think we are free men and women and live in a free society. But are we really free? Are we really freely choosing how we are and how we feel in every new moment, or are we bound by invisible chains that tie us to what we think we should be doing or attach us to our past? The truth is, unless we live totally in the present moment, with no thoughts of the past and no aspect of our character shaped by the past, we are indeed tied to it and therefore not entirely free. We all have patterns from the past: patterns of behavior, ways of thinking, ideas and fears that have been implanted in us, mostly by other people, who were also not free!

These unhelpful patterns are a major source of stuff. An example of a pattern might be that a dog bit us when we were two years old, so for the rest of our lives we are terrified of dogs. The examples are endless, and so is the amount of potential stuff we can collect over the years. As far as people whispering is concerned, the relevance of recognizing your stuff is that it clears the way for you to communicate effectively and easily with other people, because you are in a position to take responsibility for what you bring and consequently avoid cluttering your relationships.

By being aware of what triggers you to feel uncomfortable emotions or to feel physical unrest, you shine a light on the sources of your discomfort. Once this light is present, you are free from being run by the pattern because now you can see it. As you begin to identify limiting patterns in yourself and to free yourself from them, it becomes easier to recognize the stuff that is not yours when you are with another person. This in turn means that you won't fall into the trap of taking on another person's stuff as your own, which will be a great help in making your communication clearer and more valid.

So Whose Stuff Is It, Then?

Let's say you are in a challenging situation and the other person just doesn't seem to be playing ball: they even think you are in the wrong! But you are sure that they are at fault and you may even start to become quite emotional (hurt, annoyed or whatever) about it. And so do they. So, whose stuff is it? Well, the way you are feeling about it is your stuff: the way they are feeling about it is their stuff. Nobody has the monopoly on the truth. Your truth is right—for you. Their truth is equally right—for them. That can be difficult to accept.

Ask yourself:

✦ Is someone trying to nail stuff on you by saying "You did this" or "You did that" or "It's your fault" or "You made me feel like this?" People will attempt to run all kinds of guilt patterns on you if they are unable to get you to take on their stuff. Watch out for someone trying to make you feel guilty for not taking on what is theirs.

If you realize something is someone else's stuff, it may be best not to say anything about it to them. You may be taking a risk by saying anything, as the other person may not respond too well to hearing us say, "But, it's your stuff!" (Trust me; I've made that mistake myself!) The most diplomatic way is to recognize it but keep it to yourself.

Things to do:

1. Start to notice when a comment or action by someone else has a negative emotional effect on you. Realize it is your stuff that is making you feel that way: if none of your stuff resonated with what the other person said or did, it would pass through you unnoticed.

2. When you notice your stuff "come up," acknowledge it inwardly and watch the feelings you have with interest. By doing this you will have altered the dynamic and the hold it has on you.

3. Be aware of when people try to make you responsible for how they feel. It can be quite challenging not to accept that responsibility, especially with someone you care about.

4. Avoid blaming, labeling or judging either yourself or anyone else for having stuff: anyone who has no stuff will probably be no less than a real live angel, and you don't see many of those hovering around these days!

5. Laugh at your stuff: next time you recognize a pattern coming up that you have seen in yourself before, have a chuckle to yourself at it.

6. Be compassionate toward someone you see being run by their stuff: it is a way of acknowledging that we are all in the same boat in some way or other.

Difficult and Obnoxious Behavior

Sometimes we humans do challenging or mad things. We act out of character because of stress, inappropriate role models, to control others, to hide our own fears, to attract attention, out of desperation, anger, frustration or lack of direction, because of a need for love and approval, because we're going through changes or for no apparent reason whatsoever.

Difficult and obnoxious behavior comes in all shapes and sizes and can have a small irritating effect on you or can be life-threatening. It can range from being grumpy or stubborn to homicidal. We could go on and on listing ways in which humans have been found to be difficult and behave obnoxiously: our species are so creative at this kind of thing, on an individual scale as well as globally.

Personal relationships are a very fertile place for difficult behavior to grow, possibly the most fertile place of all. It may be the case that people display difficult behavior in personal relationships because they feel loved and safe, and are therefore more able to express themselves!

People whisperers know that the person is not the behavior, so they remain detached and love the person behind the behavior.

♦ Are there any people in your life who indulge in difficult or obnoxious behavior? Do you find yourself treading on eggshells in what you say or do around them? What starts them off?

♦ How is it for you when they behave obnoxiously? Notice what happens inside you when someone close to you displays difficult behavior.

♦ Would their behavior seem obnoxious to someone in a different position to you? Would their behavior seem obnoxious to them, from their point of view?

♦ Ask yourself: what are they trying to achieve or communicate through this challenging behavior? It can be easier to understand someone's behavior if you see their reasons for acting in such a way.

Dealing with Difficult or Obnoxious Behavior in Other People

If you have the option, give a person space to be obnoxious on their own and allow them to experience the consequences of their behavior. Place yourself in a position where you experience the consequences of their behavior as little as possible. You may need to be out of the way altogether for a time: everyone has times of madness, so decide how much of someone else's madness is OK for you to live with.

Expect the unexpected:
even people you know well can be unpredictable.

It is worth remembering that sometimes people who are being difficult or obnoxious are completely unaware of it. If you make them aware of it in a way they can understand, you may find they are sorry to realize how they have been behaving or affecting you.

Avoid rescuing them or changing who you are in the hope that they stop doing whatever it is that they are doing (unless you do so temporarily until you are out of danger). If you alter your behavior and they realize this, they have found a way to control you which they will almost certainly use again. Stay as centered and still as possible: respond but don't react. Quietly send them love, despite the air being thick with "challenge."

If you can, ask the person what it is that is really upsetting them? Hold the space and give them chance to express their pain without judgment or reaction. Above all, continue to love the person behind the behavior and remember that the person is not the behavior.

Dealing with Your Own Difficult or Obnoxious Behavior

Do you ever catch yourself indulging in obnoxious behavior? Who or what is it that sets you off? At what point do you realize the behavior has overtaken you, you are no longer in charge of yourself and a phantom has taken possession of you? Can you exorcise the phantom before it causes irreparable damage to your important relationships: that is, the relationships with yourself, your loved ones, other people and the universe?

Be aware of your emotions when they are still small; notice the tiny signals that your body, mind and feelings are sending to you.

Remember that it is easier to avoid being overtaken by emotions when they are still small and quiet: once they grow to a size where they take you over, they are in the driving seat.

Things to do:

1. Lie down on the imaginary psychiatrist's couch, and think about your childhood: what kinds of difficult or obnoxious behavior were happening in your home when you were young? Explore this. It is your blueprint.

2. Think of ways you behave that are difficult for yourself and for the people in your life (be honest, nobody is a saint). Think about what drives these behaviors in you: what is it you want that you are not getting?

3. Address your own difficult behavior: let your anger out in a non-harmful way if you need to. Explore ways to deal with anger: try taking up meditation or yoga, which can dissolve a lot of negative energy.

Having healthy boundaries and handling conflict effectively can be challenging at times, but the rewards in terms of the quality of your life and love are immeasurable. Fortunately, people whispering is not just about handling difficulties, it is mostly about creating joy and abundance by enjoying fantastic levels of caring and communication with your fellow human beings. It is also about creating balance for yourself, inspiring others, and connecting with the infinite universe and all it has to share with you. People whispering offers many rewards, as we will see in Part III.

PART III

Whispering
to the Universe

SECRET NINE
Balance Work, Life, Sex and Money

Arabian horses are widely admired for their beauty and intelligence. They are also well known for their incredible stamina and huge capacity for work. Early in my career with horses I was blessed to have a most wonderful Arabian mare, and I spent almost all day every day for a couple of years with her. She taught me a great deal about communicating with sensitivity. Her chestnut coat glinted in the sun, she galloped like the wind, her mane and tail flying high, and she was a loving and faithful companion.

Unfortunately, in the beginning I was so hungry to work at my horsemanship and to learn as much as I could about this subtle art, that I more than once pushed too hard and lost perspective. Usually it would be me that would suffer some pain, strain or heartache as a result of my misplaced or over-zealous efforts, but I would not be the only one to suffer, and acknowledging that my lack of balance may have caused suffering in another was one of the toughest and most humbling truths to accept.

Day in and day out I could ride this Arabian mare out across the open moors, wilderness and countryside at speed: she would go for hours, never get tired and would end the day as fresh and fit as when we started. That was fine, because that what she was born and bred to do. But alas I began to become interested in training and schooling horses to perform intricate high school movements and became quite driven. To this end I began to school my Arabian mare in many of the demanding gymnastic exercises this kind of training requires, however poorly or inaccurately I knew them.

I became very absorbed in my work of training this horse, until one morning I went to get her in from the field and she was so lame she could hardly move. My precious Arabian mare was a cripple and I was heartbroken. Normally when a horse is lame it is relatively easy to tell which leg is hurting, but in this instance it looked as though the whole horse was damaged. The veterinary surgeon looked at her and told me I may as well breed a foal from her because she was going to need a year off work. "A year off work?!"

In the back of my mind there was a thought I dare not even think at the time, or dare not admit to thinking: "What if I have caused her to be like this because of what I have been doing?" It seemed as though she had acted as a mirror for me, showing me what happens when we lose balance in our work, and she carried the physical pain of my lack of balance as evidence for me to see.

As it turned out, I was given a lucky reprieve, although I was determined to not let the lesson go unlearned. Since she was going to need a year off work, I asked the blacksmith to remove her iron shoes. While he was doing this he asked if I had thought about trying a qualified equine chiropractor as a last resort before giving her up for the year. A course of chiropractic therapy had the mare back to work within a few weeks, and as I continued my work with her thereafter, I always held the thought of what is a balanced level of work and play.

Because of a lack of balance in our lives, sometimes we suffer, and sometimes our loved ones and significant people in our lives suffer. In that situation, it was my precious Arabian mare who suffered.

People whisperers know the benefits of having every aspect of life in balance: they are committed to being centered within themselves and notice when they need to re-balance.

Our natural state is to be "in balance," where everything is effortless: we are centered and focused and everything we do falls into place with ease. Despite that, it seems quite rare for us to actually be in perfect balance. There are so many ways to be out of balance in life and it is common to spend much of our time out of balance.

We are "out of balance" when our emotions are shaky, when things do not stack up easily, when too much work has overburdened us, when life's difficulties make us uncomfortable or when our minds are overrun by distractions.

We can also be knocked off balance by good things in life, such as falling in love, coming into money or having a wild time. If we allow any of these influences to tip us too far, it can become quite difficult to right ourselves again, as the further we go off balance the harder it is to come back to being centered. The sooner we correct our auto-pilot back on to "center," the easier life can be lived.

> Balance can be lost by "overdoing it" in any way, whether it is by working, feeling, thinking or exercising too much.

Other people's influence

We can be knocked off balance by other people intentionally saying something to make us react. People may say things to control us, to get us to rescue them or fulfill a need for attention or love which they have: by knocking us out of balance they have had an effect on us and that is what they are looking for.

Sometimes we are pushed off balance by people without them meaning to, perhaps by asking too much of us and because we feel we ought to help, we over-stretch ourselves.

Our own influence

And it is not only outside influences that can knock us off center. We subject ourselves to strong desires and emotional ups and downs such as by guilt, fear, frustration or obsessive thinking.

We often over-exert ourselves, push our bodies too hard or fill them with unsuitable food, drink or drugs.

It is not selfish to be concerned about maintaining your own life balance: your efforts to stay in balance are a very generous act toward others, because when you are balanced you can give more love and support to others, since you are not using valuable energy to deal with your own lack of balance.

Being Addicted to Being Out of Balance

Bizarrely, we can become addicted to being out of balance. Being out of balance gives us something to obsess about and use to create our own personal drama. It gives us something to talk about with others and is a way to attract the attention and support of people close to us. If we are upset or struggling with a relationship, health or work-related difficulty, or someone has done something to upset us, we can really get our teeth into being unbalanced.

If you notice yourself doing this: great, you've noticed. That means you can make a choice about what is the healthiest way to continue: whether to carry on being out of balance because it benefits you or whether to find a balanced position and take responsibility for your own needs.

Balanced people can help others,
because their energy is free and honest.

If you recognize that someone close to you habitually unbalances themselves and it seems to benefit them, pointing it out may not help. Be loving and empathic, without buying into their drama by giving it energy or attention. Support them but avoid carrying their "stuff."

Realigning Your Balance

Living life skillfully is about making an almost constant string of minor (and sometimes major) corrections that bring us back into balance. This is how we unconsciously steer a car down a straight stretch of road: by tiny readjustments of the wheel. As a learner driver we leave it too late and then have to make big conscious corrections, but as experienced drivers, we keep a better line and make small unconscious corrections all the time.

The list below highlights areas where balance can be lost and suggests ways to re-balance yourself.

Emotions: Notice when your emotions rise up. If you can be aware of what is happening inside you, there is less chance of losing your balance. Stay with it and keep watching your emotions.

Thoughts: Be aware of when you think compulsively about something and your mind can't/won't stop thinking about it or let it go. Again, by noticing what is going on in your mind, you will regain your balance.

Body talk: Listen to your body: if it is tired, let it rest. If it is hungry or thirsty, give it food or drink. If it reacts badly to something (like too much alcohol, chocolate, coffee, exercise, fresh air, exhaust fumes, work, etc.), avoid exposing it to what it cannot handle. If it has excess energy to express, let it out! Run, play and dance: turn your energy loose (ideally in a way that is fun but also socially acceptable!). Illness is often a result of your body shouting at you to get it back in balance; it has probably been whispering the same message to you for a while, but it wasn't being heard.

Biting off more than you can chew: Sometimes life throws us into something that is difficult to handle and our balance disappears. But there are times when we unnecessarily enter more difficult situations or relationships than we can really handle and still maintain our balance.

STEPS TO RE-BALANCING

1. Keep your awareness on what is happening in your mind, emotions and body.

2. If possible, go somewhere quiet or be on your own. Let your body be really still and quiet: this is a great way to begin the balancing process. Let your body lead the way to stillness and allow your emotions and mind to follow your body's example.

3. It may help to take a break or put some space between you and whatever is challenging your balance, whether that is a person or a situation.

4. There is no point trying to force yourself back into balance. Being in balance is your natural state. Go into being quiet, watch your breath, give yourself space and wait . . . allow your natural balance to return.

Fun, Fun, Fun

Like balance, fun is a natural part of life, but one that we sometimes lose sight of. Fun is an excellent tool for re-balancing, helping to release the build-up of "heavy energy" caused by meeting the demands of our modern adult lifestyles. Fun and play are something that animals do even as adults, especially mammals. Watch dogs, cats, horses or even cattle: assuming their basic needs are met, they all have fun and play-times scheduled into their timetable of biorhythms.

Having fun is a great way to access the playful inner child which we all carry within us somewhere. Recognizing our inner child and letting it out to play helps to put things into perspective in our lives. Sharing fun with others is a fabulous way of creating or deepening bonds. Laughing together and reaching the lighter parts of life with someone is very healing and a great way to lower barriers between people.

Some questions for you about fun:

Everyone has their own ideas about what is fun: what is your idea of fun?

Be honest with yourself about what is really fun for you.

What do you think of as acceptable ways to have fun?

Choose from anything that is legal and doesn't harm anyone!

What fun things would you try if you had the chance or if you dare?

Within the next six months, go ahead and do one fun thing you've never done before and wished you had.

Can you have too much fun?

You may say you could never have too much fun, and in many ways that is a great attitude to have in life, but if the need for fun becomes an addiction, like anything else, it may become a source of loss of balance.

Are you afraid of what others might think?

Our own judgments about what might be seen as a frivolous or childish activity can stop us from having fun. Notice if you are not having fun as you would like because of what others—or yourself—might think: go ahead, do it and be empowered by not giving a damn if you look a fool or not!

Things to do:

1. Notice the next time you have one of those (probably) rare moments when you experience a sense of being totally in balance. Explore it, cherish it, indulge in it, be with it and let yourself become deeply familiar with it, so that you will be able to re-create it at other times.

2. Create a list of five people or situations that can knock you out of balance easily. Use this awareness to help you be prepared and centered when you are in that company or situation again.

3. Set aside regular times to re-balance yourself by having a break, resting and having fun. This could be for thirty minutes a day, one day a week, one week a year—whatever it takes for you.

4. Avoid doing too much of anything: work, worrying, thinking, eating, emotional roller coaster rides, giving and not receiving etc.

5. Within the next six months, go ahead and do one fun thing you've never done and wished you had.

Sex

Sex is one of the deepest and most wonderful ways for people to communicate and exchange energies. It is a natural and effective way to release energy, re-balance, connect with another person and have fun all at the same time. Unlike most other species, humans have been given the gift of sex not only to procreate, but also to enjoy as a means of connecting with one another.

Sex is an emotive subject, not least because it is such a powerful force within us. Since it is such a powerful force, many religions and societies have felt the need to control sex and give it a certain taboo. Unfortunately, this kind of cultural control of what is an instinctive and natural way to connect with each other has brought much fear, guilt and discomfort with it. Despite that, it remains as popular as ever (funny that!) and continues to bring much-needed intimacy into people's lives.

Sex can be reduced to a functional, physical activity, but at its best, it can be one of the most rewarding ways to communicate with another person. There is little disagreement that sex within the context of a loving, intimate relationship is more deeply fulfilling than just plain sex.

Depending on your beliefs and attitudes around the subject, sex can be many things:

Sex can be awesome.

Sex can be gentle.

Sex can be a relief.

Sex can be playful.

Sex can be uplifting.

Sex can be loving.

Sex can be beautiful.

Sex can make you feel open.

Sex can make you feel vulnerable.

Sex can be selfish.

Sex can be wild.

Sex can be lonely.

Sex can be moving.

Sex can be painful.

Sex can be passionate.

Sex can be boring.

Sex can be exciting.

Sex can make you feel closed.

Sex can be disturbing.

Sex can be funny.

Let's Talk About Sex

Because sex can be a taboo, embarrassing or uncomfortable subject to discuss, people don't always talk about their needs in a direct and understandable way. As a result of this, they can continue to feel disappointed with their sex lives. It may take courage to speak up and ask your partner to turn you on by wearing a cutesy pink tutu, yelling like Tarzan and swinging from the wardrobe door before kissing your fingertips and saying "I am yours," but hey, if that's what you need to get you going, you had better ask for it, because no one is going to be able to do that much guesswork for you!

Starting to talk about a subject such as sex is often the hardest part. Once you and your partner know that it is safe and OK to communicate openly about the subject, you will be able to move forward together to new heights of experience.

WHAT DOES SEX MEAN TO YOU?

✦ Do you feel more in touch with your partner during sex or do you experience a separation from them?

✦ Do you have a partner who does things in ways that help you to feel more connected and in ways you like?

✦ Do you ask for what you want from your partner in a way they understand?

✦ Have you asked your partner what they would like from you?

✦ Do you feel more loved or less loved before, during and after sex?

✦ Do you help your partner feel loved during sex?

✦ Do you have sex with your whole self—body, mind and soul— or just your genitals?

Guiding Your Lover

It is most effective to teach your partner what you want from them by communicating through positive responses. Whenever they do something you like, phrases such as "Mmm, that's good" or "I love it when you do that" will guide them and help to create the kind of experiences you want to have. People usually resist learning if they receive negative responses: especially so when they are very open and vulnerable, such as during lovemaking (and especially if a man receives a negative response in this situation!). Negative responses might be phrases such as "that's not very good," or "I don't like that." A lover can feel easily hurt and will very soon giving up searching for ways to please you if they receive too many of those comments. (That does not mean you cannot put boundaries in place if what is happening is not OK for you).

So be sure to talk in a way that frames things in the positive: that means saying things like, "This really turns me on" or "That feels good to me" and avoid criticism of your partner or they may close down very quickly. Remember that sex is a sensitive area for most people, so they can feel very vulnerable to negative feedback or criticism.

The best timing for giving positive feedback is to respond in the moment. For example, if your lover's hand is somewhere you like, an approving sound from you will teach them they are on the right track. If they do something that isn't right for you, don't say "no"—just be quiet. This is a very clear way of teaching someone what works and what doesn't for you, and subsequently for them too.

Most people want to please; they just need some help and encouragement in figuring out how. Of course some people are more receptive and quicker learners than others, so don't get impatient if your guiding or training doesn't get immediate results. If the way you are communicating isn't working, look for different ways to put across the same idea.

Ask yourself about sex:

✦ What signals do you give out about yourself sexually through your body language, the way you are and the

things you say? How do you think other people read the
signals that you give out?

✦ What expectations do you have around sex? Are these
expectations realistic?

✦ Does sex cause you discomfort because of the fear of losing control of yourself or your feelings? Is that because the
sensations of sex are overwhelming and it means someone
else may take control of you?

✦ If you are in a relationship, what are you communicating
to yourself or to your partner that may not be helping
your sex life together? What ways could you communicate
to yourself or your partner that might be more helpful?

Making Love with Your Whole Self

What we are talking about here is communicating sexually with
another person, but going beyond the body. As with every other
aspect of people whispering, communicating through sex can
also take place on many different levels. It doesn't take much to
have sex with just your essential physical parts, but then it does-
n't always give you much back either. Engaging the whole of
yourself—body, mind and soul—when making love with your
partner will help both of you to reach greater heights of connection and intimacy.

To engage the whole of your body, focus on the different sensations in different parts of your body: sense what you feel in
your legs, feet, head, chest or hands simultaneously during lovemaking. Let your awareness take you deeper into the experiences
that your body is leading you through. To physically engage the
whole of your partner, touch not only their body, but particularly
their head, face and hair. People live mostly in their heads and
feel that is where "they" are, so connecting with their head can
help them feel you are paying attention to them "personally." To
completely connect with someone's whole body, try touching
your lover's feet during lovemaking. This may make them feel as

if their body is being totally embraced by you, literally from head to toe (not forgetting the interesting bits in the middle of course).

Become sensitive to timing and moods:
work with the nature of sexuality, rather than against it.

To connect with your lover on a deeper level, look into their eyes during lovemaking. Remember that the eyes are the windows of the soul and this can intensify the sense of togetherness you both experience.

Be as present as possible with your partner: that means being aware of everything that is happening in you, between you and around you. It means dropping thoughts about whether to have chicken or beef for dinner, where to go on vacation or what to tell the neighbors in order to explain away all your squeals. It also means dropping fantasies about being with someone else or somewhere else. When you drop all the mental interference and are totally there in the moment, you open up the possibility of a far richer level of communicating experience for both yourself and your partner, since when you are fully present, they will sense it and be able to join you.

Things to do:
1. Enjoy yourself! Explore sex as a means of experiencing a variety of deep physical, mental, spiritual and fun connections with another human.
2. Ask yourself honest questions about what sex means to you and where those meanings come from.
3. Bite the bullet and start to find ways to have honest, open conversations about sex. Ask for what you want in ways that make it easy for your lover to want to respond.
4. Start training your partner using positive guidance: think of it as a long-term project. On the one hand you focus on how their training is coming along; on the other hand, you focus on your skills as a trainer and communicator.

Money

Along with sex, money is an area of our lives that can have a big influence on our state of balance. Money could be the subject of a whole book in itself (and probably is), but what we are specifically looking at here is money as a form of communication between people.

Money is an amazing and often contentious concept that is all about people: without people, money simply would not exist. Money represents an agreement between people, a way of exchanging energy at a pre-agreed rate. Money is not really about paper, copper or gold; it represents our efforts and is a way of swapping one person's efforts for those of another person.

> Money may not be the answer to life's problems, but I have heard it said that money is a great lubricator in life!

Money is a means for the universe and other people to provide for us, so we can live our lives without having to do everything for ourselves. In the West, we no longer have to grow all our own food, build our own houses or provide for our other needs entirely ourselves. The wonderful medium of money enables people to support each other so they are free to pursue more varied and expressive lives, knowing their particular contribution to society means they don't have to take care of all of their basics first-hand. People whisperers enjoy the mechanism of money as a way for people to exchange their energies: they allow it to flow freely, trusting the universe to provide.

Some views about money

Money is seen:

✦ to cause trouble between people, but it is not the money that causes the trouble, it is the people

✦ to be the answer to our problems, but the problems exist in our minds, because we perceive a gap between how we want things to be and how they actually are in reality

✦ to make us comfortable. There is no doubt money can buy you a more comfortable hospital bed, but it won't necessarily make the pain in your body hurt any less

✦ to buy us a good life, but it cannot mend a broken heart, bring back a loved one or create inner fulfillment

✦ to afford us freedom: freedom from having to work, freedom to travel and to do the things we want to do; but true freedom is a state of mind and comes for free anyway

✦ to bring us security, but it cannot save us from being a danger to ourselves. Besides, security is something of an illusion: you could have all the money in the world and your private jet could "plop" into the ocean never to be seen again!

Allowing money to balance and flow

So if money represents an exchange of energy and effort between people, what is happening if money is not flowing easily into your life (or into your pocket)? Could it be you are withholding your energy from someone, or is someone withholding their energy from you? Have a look at other areas of your life other than just money, e.g. relationships: areas where you might be wasting energy, blocking energy, investing or expending it in non-worthwhile ways or allowing it to be drained from you. Does each area of your life give you a reasonable return for the investment of energy you put in?

> If you are fortunate enough to have lots of money, saving it all up in a fearful way could interfere with its flow, and energy that is not flowing is not serving or creating anything.

If you do what you are passionate about and allow things to flow, the money will follow. But doing something just for the fun of it and not for payment is not necessarily likely to bring you money: it is a hobby, not a paid job. In order to receive money for doing something you love, you have to communicate to other people or the universe that you are happy to be paid for your services. You also need to be clear with yourself that your work has value and believe you deserve to be paid for it.

Money as a positive exchange

Do you appreciate the money you have coming in? If you do, more will probably follow. Since money is a way for people to exchange their energies, appreciating the money that you have is similar to expressing your appreciation of another person's efforts on your behalf, which will make them want to do more for you. If every time you do a job your primary motivation is your love of the job, you will do the job to a higher standard and people will notice this; then more people will want to hire you and more money will flow to you.

> When money is handed over from one person to another it can be a loving exchange or a negative exchange: choose to make it the former.

Ask yourself:

✦ Which do you notice most—the people who have more money than you or the people who have less? How does this affect your take on life?

✦ Do you enjoy exchanging money with people as a way of saying thanks for them giving you their energy or helping you? Do you allow money to flow freely in your life?

✦ What do you really need other than food, shelter and basic medical care? Can you think of all the rest as a fantastic bonus?

ADAM AND NICKY'S STORY

Adam and Nicky were a successful professional couple in their late twenties. They both earned good money, worked hard, played hard, owned their own home, and were very happy together and very much in love. Then, after about two years of living and enjoying their life together to the full, the company Adam worked for was hit by the dotcom crash and he was laid-off from his job. As he was a high flyer he had no trouble finding new employment. In fact, he found a placement that was actually going to further his career more than his previous post could have done.

The only down side of Adam's new job was it was more than two hundred miles away from where they lived, and Nicky's job in publishing was tied to their original location. Aside from which, they both loved where they lived and didn't have any desire to move. So Adam commuted to work during the week and came back home at weekends.

This arrangement worked OK for the first year or so, but as time went on Nicky began to feel the strain of snatching a few hours of intimacy at the weekends. And even those few hours at weekends were not giving them any real quality time together. Adam would arrive home very late on Friday evenings and was then tired out all day Saturday. Because he used to drive off again on Sunday evening to get ready for work on Monday morning, he would spend the whole of Sunday feeling tense and unable to relax, in anticipation of going again. Nicky explained to me in one of our coaching sessions how she felt more and more unloved and isolated in her relationship. After two years of this arrangement, her need for more intimacy led to her becoming interested in another man, and wondering whether to leave Adam in order to begin a new relationship with the other man.

Nicky and Adam had allowed work and money to push them apart. They had lost the balance in their lives and forgotten how important their relationship was and how much fun they had together. I asked Nicky if she had communicated how she felt to Adam in a way he understood and she replied she didn't think he realized what was going on—so probably not. I suggested she talk to Adam by speaking his language, using words and phrases he would understand, and she also hold the space and give him time to say how it was for him, without fear of a reaction.

They did talk about their situation and, as a result, when Nicky heard Adam's point of view, she realized just how inflexible she had been in sticking with her job when Adam had been forced to move on. As a result of this, she spoke to her employers who agreed to her working on a freelance basis from home, which meant that she would earn less money but have more free time. It also meant that they would be able to move their home to where Adam's work was based, thereby regaining the balance in their life and relationship at long last.

> Enjoy money as much as possible, but remember to keep it in perspective and take a balanced approach to it. However much you have or don't have, it is all temporary and you can't take it with you when you die anyway.

Things to do:

1. Start to enjoy money without becoming emotionally needy, knocked off balance or overly attached to it (no one said all the suggestions in this book were going to be easy!). Experiment with letting money flow in your life. This means being aware of how you allow it in and out of your life and the emotions you attach to those comings and goings.

2. Look at people who are successful or simply comfortable with money. Study how they think, act and feel that makes money work for them.

3. Think about the underlying need that would be met if you had all the money you wanted . . . would it be security, comfort, enjoyment, approval, etc?

Work

Work is a very interesting thing: it is viewed in so many different ways by so many people. Work is one of the major areas where people whisperers can practice their art and thrive as a result of skillful communication. Work is almost entirely about other people, involving either talking to customers or dealing with managers, fellow staff or bosses. Much of our experience and success at work is about our interaction with others.

Work is one of the areas of life that is closely related to money and frequently knocks us off balance. "Work" is a major four-letter word and one that takes up a huge amount of time in our lives. Our beliefs about work are highly significant in determining the quality of the lives that we enjoy, or don't enjoy. Work can be one of the most fulfilling and motivating aspects of your life or it can be one of the most difficult and tedious areas.

> If we weren't meant to work, there would be piles of food left out for us every morning by the food fairies, homes would build themselves, and all our other needs, wants and entertainments would be met just by asking (actually, that doesn't sound too bad!).

Work can play a large part in expressing who you are, which is why people whisperers seek to work in fulfilling ways that make a valuable contribution to others, as well as to themselves.

Ask yourself:

✦ How do you see your work? Do you work for money or for the love of what you do? Would you dare to think you could work for the latter?

✦ How do you view other people in work? Have you ever made assumptions about people because of the work they do?

✦ If work brings meaning to our days, what meaning do you allow your work to bring to your days?

✦ Do you see the work you do as bringing value to the people who are at the receiving end of your products or services, e.g. the people who drink your beer, whose savings are increased by your company or who enjoy your soap at bath time?

Taking your "whole self" to work

There may be aspects of yourself—your talents, thoughts and feelings—that you don't take to work, and if you are not true to yourself at work, you may be holding yourself back from realizing your true potential. You are free to bring all of yourself to your work: that means all of your attention, energy, focus, imagination and people skills. If you were to bring your whole self to your work, most likely you would feel happier and freer, whatever workplace culture you find yourself in.

Think about how you are in the workplace. Now think about how you are in your social circle or with loved ones. How do you differ and in which situation are you happiest? Do you realize that in all of these different situations, the common factor is you?! You may find it hard to believe, but ultimately you do have choices about the work you do and how you feel about it.

Ask yourself:

✦ What parts of yourself, aspects of your personality and attitudes do you take to work with you?

✦ What parts of you do you not take to work?

✦ What do you do with the parts of yourself that you don't think you take to work?

✦ Are you someone different in the workplace than at home?

✦ What would happen if you fully engaged with what you do at work?

✦ What if you were at your most brilliant, joyful, committed and friendly when you were at work?

Myths about workplace culture

Wherever you work, there will be some kind of culture, approach, atmosphere and attitude that goes with the territory. It is very easy to think that the culture is "the company" and is therefore out of your hands. In truth, the culture is whatever the people within the company agree to buy into—and that includes you. In fact, we could go so far as to say that the company only exists as an agreement between all the people who work there at any one time. A company is a group of companions; in a commercial context they are agreeing to produce certain goods or supply certain services together. The culture and the company are not separate from you: you are a part of them and you continue to keep them alive (or not!).

How do you view your own ability to change things at work? Do you realize that you really matter, you do count and your contribution is necessary? Why else would you be paid to do what you do?

Relationships in the workplace

Your success at work depends to a huge degree on your ability to nurture relationships in the workplace. A large part of life can be spent at work, so it is beneficial to get along well together and enjoy healthy exchanges of energy. Many of the tools and skills talked about in this book will alter your work relationships, your sense of happiness, your environment and success if you apply them.

No one is an island, which means if you change your way of thinking or being, your environment and the people around you also change, even if those changes are only in the way you view things. Regardless of your rank, that means it is possible to influence people in the workplace upward and sideways as well as downward. In reality, everyone makes a difference, including you.

Influence is something that spreads out in all directions,
so don't doubt it goes upward too!

You can outgrow a limiting situation where superiors don't allow you to expand: maybe because they are too fearful to let you grow. If you outgrow your present situation you can be confident that another, more suitable situation will present itself soon for you.

Things to do:

1. Imagine that you are an old man or woman, sitting in your favorite chair. Think about what you might like to have achieved if you looked back over your life: what contribution you would like to have made, how much fun you would you have had doing it and what kind of relationships would you need around you to bring it about.

2. Ask yourself what work you would do if money were no object and you could choose anything. Dare to think it: and dare to ask what you could do to allow it to happen anyway.

3. Look at some of the work-related relationships you have: begin to make a difference for the better to one of those work relationships today.

4. Look at how much balance you have between your work and the rest of your life. How much time and energy is left over after work has taken what it needs?

5. Explore what happens if you bring all of yourself to your work: that means all of your attention, energy, focus, imagination and people skills.

To enjoy flowing communication and fulfilling relationships, it is essential to pay attention to your state of balance, which is the natural way for you to be. When you balance the different aspects of your life, including work, fun, sex and money, everything becomes effortless: the way you connect with yourself and others happens with more ease. By achieving balance in your own life you create a foundation upon which to create and share the relationships you want with other people, as we shall explore in the next secret.

SECRET TEN
Share the Path to Success

I was once presented with a horse with a "problem" that is common among horses who have worked in riding-school establishments. This kind of problem occurs in people too, whether they are people at work, the kids, husband or whoever. The horse was a beautiful black Irish thoroughbred mare. She was lazy, hard to motivate and she had gone sour in her work. Some horses that get tired of being ridden take to bucking or running off, and some take to getting so sluggish that they refuse to move anymore. This horse was the latter type. Horses express themselves through movement, so when a horse gives up the desire to move, it is almost giving up the desire for life.

Many years before this, one of my master riding teachers had taught me how to "put horses forward," which meant releasing their energy by *allowing* them to really move; so up until this time, I had never struggled to get horses moving, even lazy horses that other people found hard to motivate. This horse was different. Even the skills I had learned previously did not help me to motivate her; what I needed to do was find a way to work with her and find a win-win solution that was right for both of us. I knew this horse was not old or unwell; she was in her prime years and in good physical health, she was very active and would play around when out in the pasture with her horse friends.

The first thing I noticed when I started work was that she even resented having the saddle placed on her back. It took a great deal of time and patience to lift the saddle over her back without her threatening me and snapping in my direction with her teeth. Eventually, she realized I was not going to hurt her with the saddle, so I mounted up. I asked her to "walk on" and it was like she was made of cold treacle; she would move, but it was slow, resentful, resistant and lifeless. Nothing I did improved things at all; on each day's ride she would be resistant and half dead underneath me. She felt sour and joyless and it was making me feel the same. It was depressing and heartbreaking, as well as incredibly frustrating, to think that a fine horse such as this had lost her will to move.

Since I was getting nowhere fast with this horse, literally, I took a few days off from working with her to give myself time to think. Asking the right question was the key to this challenge, and it seemed that the right question was this: what does she want right now? The answer didn't seem very helpful, because the answer was that she wanted to be left alone and ridden as little as possible. So the next time I worked with her I gave her what she wanted: I mounted, asked her to walk only a few yards, stopped, stroked her neck, dismounted, took off the saddle and turned her out with her friends. I literally rode her as little as possible!

Day two I did the same thing.

Day three I walked her twenty yards, stopped, turned around, walked only another twenty yards, stopped, stroked her, climbed off and turned her out again.

Day four I was still in the process of climbing on-board and she rapidly started walking off by her own choice, freely and willingly. After twenty yards I stopped her, my chest bursting with joy. That was the end of her being sour and unwilling to move with me. She knew we were sharing something, that our time together would be spent aiming at win-win solutions and that I wasn't going to push or force her; the fact is that from that day she offered me whatever I asked for. Rather than trying to motivate or get her to "work," I would ask questions such as "what does she want out of this?"

I lost touch with that horse for a year or two after I had worked with her and heard that she had been sold on. One day I had a phone call out of the blue from a lady asking if I knew anything about a black Irish mare, as someone had told her I had once worked with it. She was the new owner of the horse, and told me she had a great one-to-one relationship with her. She was an experienced, knowledgeable and caring horse person who was delighted with the horse—she said the horse was willing, jumped like a stag, competed and won, and was loving and great with the kids.

People whisperers understand the value of sharing life's successes with other people: they know that by sharing, the potential for their own love, joy and success is multiplied.

Creating Win-Wins

A "win-win" is an outcome or result where everyone walks away a winner, happy and satisfied; all concerned feel they have benefited in a way that works for them. This is in contrast to outcomes where one person wins and the other loses, consequently feeling dissatisfied or denied something. Because humans can be very competitive creatures, we tend to lose sight of the potential cost of winning over someone else and forget the value of creating win-win situations.

Win-wins promote growth, opportunities,
positive energy and sharing.

Win-wins are a way to create allies: People with whom you create win-wins are more likely to stand by you in the future. They know they can work with you and you will consider their needs as well as your own.

Win-wins create positive energy: There is a feel-good factor when people create a win-win.

Win-wins create the possibility of new levels of relationship: By creating a win-win, you form a bond of mutual respect with the other person.

Win-wins create a sense of sharing: Win-win solutions make both parties feel cared for and important.

Win-wins bring the possibility of new creativity and opportunities: Because win-wins are about building bridges and creating new or renewed relationships, there is the chance of taking your relationships into new areas.

Win-wins send the right kind of boomerang words and actions out into the universe: Since win-wins are a positive and loving way to communicate with people, they send out loving and positive energy, which will return to you sooner or later. Every time you create a win-win with someone, that person takes the positive energy with them out into the world and furthers your cause as a result.

How to Create Win-Wins

✦ Set things up to be easy: the fewer obstacles you put in the way of finding a smooth flow that both parties can share, the better.

✦ Let go of anger, frustration or any other negative emotion and the need to be right at all costs. This is easy to say and not so easy to do, especially when you feel strongly about the issue or you start digging into your position and don't want to budge.

✦ Put yourself in the other person's shoes. See what they need to gain from a resolution. See what is making it difficult for them, and see where you can soften to allow more room for them to move, especially if they have boxed themselves into a corner.

✦ Ask the other person and/or your inner self what the options are, or what else could help to make everyone a winner. Think of at least three options, even if only one of them seems realistic!

✦ Use your imagination to allow solutions to grow. Our minds are mostly limited to thinking of things we have already thought of, so allow your mind to be quiet and let your imagination fill the space with new ideas.

✦ Let go of any specific expectations you have about the result: there may be a number of ways in which you could gain what you need. By letting go of what the outcome should be, you widen the gap of possibilities. Remember, whatever happens, none of this will matter to you in a hundred years' time, so why not let go of some of it now?

✦ See if giving the other person/people what they want in some way gets you what you want. It may not work that way, but sometimes, by giving, the other person will give too.

✦ In a difficult situation, ask the other party, "How can we resolve it?" (rather than *you or I*).

Things to do:

1. Simple: look for opportunities to create win-wins! That way you can't lose!

2. Open yourself to possibilities instead of digging into your own position.

3. Stand back from the situation: if you look at any relationship problem from a different angle it will look different and will certainly feel different.

4. Imagine a life in which all of your close companions are winners, winning in win-wins . . . In what ways would your life differ from the way it is now? What would it take to make that imagined life a reality?

5. Most importantly: be a gracious and good loser. That way you can't lose. We can't win them all, and sometimes there are surprising and amazing benefits to losing!

6. Be aware of when you think you are creating a win-win, but you are actually creating a win-lose—in which you are the loser! This isn't being kind or charitable on your part, it is being a fool.

The Power of Questions

You have probably noticed by now that this book has lots of questions for you to answer: that's because there is only one person in the universe who has all the answers you need, and that is YOU. Asking yourself the questions in this book and answering them will certainly move you forward, so be caring toward yourself and answer them. Don't just read the questions and skip over them. You'll be amazed at what you find out about your life, loves, relationships and yourself—from yourself!

One of the most powerful tools for creating success in life is our ability to ask good questions. It is undoubtedly those people in history who asked great questions who have helped the human race to move forward the most. The quality of the questions you ask creates the life you want to live. Everything starts with a question, so if you ask great questions, you stand far more chance of creating great answers.

Until about 6,000 years ago, humans only used to hunt and eat horses. I have often wondered who the first person was to ask the question "I wonder if I could ride on the back of one of these fast, powerful horse creatures?" The nations who asked and answered that question went on to conquer and rule most of the world, right up until the arrival of the combustion engine. That was an incredibly powerful question.

Asking Other People Questions

Asking questions in the right way opens up huge possibilities in your interactions with people in all kinds of circumstances. By asking someone something in a genuine way, you let them know you are genuinely interested in them. People can find this helpful irresistible, delightful or, because they are not used to someone showing them this level of interest, they may even feel uncomfortable and shy.

Asking questions can bring about incredible answers: sometimes, asking the right question at the right time will enable someone to find an answer they didn't even know consciously themselves before the answer came out of them. Asking genuine questions and waiting for the answer by truly listening is a way of showing love to a fellow human.

The right question always leads to the right answer.

Asking Yourself Questions

You don't only benefit by asking other people questions: asking yourself the right questions can lead you to all the information and keys you need to create the life you wish for. By asking yourself questions which you don't think you know the answers to, you bring your all-knowing unconscious mind into use. The unconscious mind is your mainframe computer; it stores everything that has ever happened to you, even though you don't think you can remember. It is also connected to the master mainframe computer, the universe, and when asked the right question, can sometimes come up with staggering answers, the like of which you could never have known "yourself." Try it. Remember that questions raised at this kind of level are not usually answered in words or thoughts made up of words, the answers normally appear somehow in life, and they appear in their own time too!

Asking the Universe Questions

You can take this a stage further; not only can you ask other people and yourself questions, you can ask questions directly to the universe, the infinite, the divine, God or however you want to think of it. You have nothing to lose. Putting questions out there is the same as putting any other word, thought or action out there: it will be answered in some way. Ask a question and an answer will come back. . . although perhaps not in the way you expected it!

Ways to Ask Brilliant Questions . . .

The whole point of asking questions is to bring about an answer, so it is important that questions are asked in a way that makes them easy to answer. Here are some ways to ask brilliant questions.

1. Always ask questions of others or of yourself that frame things positively, e.g. "What can we do to get along better together?" rather than "What do we do that makes us keep fighting?"

2. Ask questions that begin with the words "which," "how," "when," "where," etc., but avoid using the word "why" in your question. Now you're wondering *why* to avoid that word aren't you? The word "why" can imply a judgment, and may make the person who is asked more defensive. In effect the word "why" can make it harder for the person to answer the question, since they are unconsciously expecting to be judged:

   e.g. *"Why. . . did you stay late at work with your secretary?"*
   "Why. . . did you say I was a selfish lover in front of my friends?"
   "Why. . . did you steal those apples from next door's tree?"
   "Why. . . did you sink all our savings into that crashed investment company?"

3. Ask questions that come from your heart, not just from your head.

4. Make your questions easy to understand, so that the other person can focus on their answer, not on what the hell the questions meant.

5. Ask questions without emotion in your voice. Otherwise, it would be easy for the other person to hear the emotion more than the question.

6. Remember that you may think you know the answer to the question you are asking, but the answer you have in mind may not be the right answer for the other person: everyone has their own answers to life's questions.

7. Ask the right question and the answer will appear. There is a Buddhist idea that the answer is always contained within the question: it is, but it does require exactly the right question to be asked!

8. When you ask someone a question, wait for the answer and listen to it. Hold the space: immerse yourself in being quiet and pay full attention to the person who is answering.

9. Avoid questions that make the person answering feel blamed or accused of being wrong or "bad."

Things to do:

1. Try this experiment for finding something lost or mislaid, such as your car keys: think specifically about what you want to find and ask yourself when you had them last. Then ask yourself "Where did I put ——," or "What did I do with —— last?" Completely avoid saying or thinking anything negative along the lines of "I have lost it" or "I don't know where it is," etc. Relax and let the answer come to you: you may find yourself going over to the object you lost without even thinking about it. Your unconscious knows all the answers; you simply have to ask the question in a way that it can answer. Now use the same technique to manifest answers to the bigger questions in your life.

2. Start noticing the kind of questions you ask yourself on a daily basis, about your work, your relationships and your life in general. Think about reframing questions so you get more favorable answers.

3. Ask people questions in ways that help them to express themselves more constructively when they are around you.

4. Realize that questions are a huge power behind creating your experiences and the quality of all that happens to you. Use the power of questions to create whatever you want . . . no one

would have invented the light bulb, the combustion engine, the wheel or the condom if they hadn't asked a few questions first!

Ambition and Drive

Creating any kind of win, whether it is for you, someone else or for everybody requires energy to be channeled in the right way. Two effective ways to do that are through ambition and drive. People whisperers know the value of using ambition and drive as ways to further their success and they enjoy helping others to be successful too.

Ambition and Drive
Contribute to the Greatness of Humankind

It is because of our natural bent for furthering ourselves that humans have come so far in advancing our society and our way of life. It is humankind's habitual ambition that motivates us to create, invent, explore, discover and learn. Ambitious people have always been at the frontline of moving us forward to new areas of our potential, both individually and collectively.

When ambition is healthy it is a great motivator and encourages a flow of energy through us that is highly constructive: ambition could be described as the desire to fulfill our greatest potential in life, whatever that may be.

> Whoever you are and whatever stage you are at in life, there will always be new ways for you to create, invent, explore, discover and learn.

The admiration of ambition

Ambition is a greatly admired quality, especially in Western society. We tend to be very enthusiastic and supportive of people who "go for it" and make things happen in their lives. Ambitious people who rise up from humble beginnings are held in particularly high esteem. The idea of the self-made man or woman, who dragged themselves up from the backstreets to go on to greatness, is something we hold up as an ideal.

This is fine if you are ambitious: but if you lack ambition and drive or don't know where your real purpose in life yet lies, it can be very disheartening. There is a sense in our society that being ambitious is the right thing, and not being ambitious implies there is something wrong.

Whatever you feel passionate about,
whatever you feel driven to do, follow that path.

Following Your Dreams:
Finding Your True Purpose

Once you find the things in life that are "on purpose" for you, the things that really trigger your ambition, there comes a powerful flow of ready energy with which you can supply your drive. Something that absorbs you will allow them to go on way past normal human effort or endeavor.

What may be stopping you from living your dreams?

✦ **Patience.** It may be that the time has not yet come for you to harvest your ambitious energy; there may be other aspects of life or other people that need to come into your life before your true purpose becomes obvious.

✦ **Honesty.** Because of the negative influences of the people in our lives, it can be quite difficult to be really honest with ourselves about exactly what we would really love to do with our lives.

✦ **Letting go of limiting beliefs.** Many people know what they would love to do, but don't attempt it because of all sorts of limiting beliefs. They believe they have to stay where they are because of commitments, duty, or habit, or because maybe they wouldn't be good enough to "cut it." It may take huge courage to go for doing the thing you would love to do with your life: there is risk involved in letting go of what is familiar and following your ambitions and dreams. Often, the gifts you receive are in direct proportion to the size of the risk and trust you are prepared to have.

Nurturing Ambition and Drive in Yourself and Other People

In order to nurture ambition we need to offer positive encouragement, yet without letting our own agenda interfere. For example, the parents of an ambitious child may start out by simply encouraging them, but then find themselves beginning to push the child for their own satisfaction. We also need to create space for ambition to be pursued without too many distractions, to give whatever support is needed (including supporting ourselves) and to strike a good balance so that other areas of life enhance the area of ambition.

Things to do:

1. Think about some of the peak moments and personal achievements in your life. Think about what you did to bring them about.

2. What really turns you on now? What would you love to be doing, or doing more of that you would so easily be able to commit your energy to? Go ahead and do it.

3. Think about your ambitions in relation to those close to you: are your ambitions really for you or for them?

4. Whenever you are pursuing your ambition, notice if you are totally absorbed in it, or if you have negative feelings about whether you "should" be doing it. Do you feel that you "should" be doing the housework or getting on with a project or paying

the bills instead? You are here on earth for a few short years, so choose to do the things that will make the most valuable contribution and difference, and when you are doing them, commit yourself totally.

5. Commit yourself to following your ambition, but be aware if you start to "push" and therefore creating possible resistance to good outcomes.

6. Focus on your ambitions: enjoy the ready supply of energy that comes to you when you pursue your ambition.

7. Support other people in pursuing their ambitions in ways they need, not in ways that you think they need. To know the difference between the two, ask what would help them the most.

Delegating and Motivating

No matter how self-sufficient you might be in life, there are countless ways in which you rely on other people and need them to perform tasks for you. This may be something direct like asking someone in your family to do something in the home, asking a colleague to do something in the workplace, or it may be a service such as getting your car fixed or booking a decent massage. It may mean getting someone to arrange a special blind date for you or asking someone to clinch a billion-dollar deal.

So to share the path to success, it is helpful to be good at delegating and motivating other people. People whisperers understand the importance of asking other people for help in ways that work: they trust everyone's unique ability to play their part, and motivate people with energy, balance and inspiration.

> Never be afraid to directly and openly ask for help or advice when you need it: the worst thing the other person can say is "no."

It is a fun exercise to look at any aspect of your life and think how many people have contributed and helped you to be doing what you are doing. Something we take for granted, like driving a car, relies on an almost infinite number of people to put you there: the people that built the car, designed the car, supplied the materials for the car, who supplied the rubber for the tires, the ranch-hand who looked after the cattle that supplied the leather for the seats, the people who built the car plant, who feed the car workers, who grow the food to supply the car-plant canteen, transporters who carried the materials, sales team that sold the car . . . oh well, this could go on forever. The fact is that we all rely on other people to do things for us to a huge degree.

Asking for Help

You simply cannot do everything yourself: you have to ask others for help. The best way to ask for help is to ask in very plain language; when you have the person's attention; in a way they understand and without "loading" the way you ask with a negative emotional charge. Phew—that sounds like a challenge!

Asking for something with a negative emotional charge means there is anger, frustration, force, control, over-use of power, "apologetic-ness," desperation, hope or any other kind of unhelpful energy in your voice, the words you use and your body language.

Ideally, ask from a place of detachment, where you are clear about what you want and it will not affect your emotional state whether it is complied with or not by the other person.

If you delegate to someone with an emotion such as anger in you, even if you attempt to hide the anger they will feel it, so when they carry out the task it will be tainted by that emotion.

If someone understands the reason or value of doing something, they are more likely to be happy to do it.

Building relationships

In order to achieve the best response when motivating or delegating, take the time to build rapport first. Imagine making a "delegation sandwich," in which the request is the filling, and relationship/rapport is the bread wrapped around that request, so that the person receiving the request gets a bite of relationship with every mouthful: before, during and after the task! Be sure to round off any delegation by revisiting your rapport and relationship with the other person after the task is completed: showing appreciation is always worthwhile.

Remember it is entirely the free choice of the other person whether they do what we ask or not; by and large we cannot make them. Even if they are an employee of ours, they can still choose not to do what is asked of them; although it is up to them to handle the consequences of that choice, of course.

Ask and let go

Once you have delegated something to someone and they have understood your request, give them room to carry out your request without you "getting in the way." It requires inner strength on your part to allow for the possibility of mistakes to be made. That can be difficult, especially if a $10 million contract rests upon it. But then, if the task is that important and you don't trust anyone else to do it, perhaps you would be better off doing it yourself in the first place, and not delegating at all. That way, if you blow the $10 million contract, you only have to forgive yourself!

Handling Mistakes

If you are secure about delegating and giving people room to get on with it while allowing them to make mistakes, the next level of challenge for you is not to reprimand them for mistakes. Generally speaking, people aren't stupid (if you are delegating important stuff to people you think are stupid, perhaps you need to ask yourself a few questions about yourself!). Provided they are aware of the consequences of their mistake, they usually realize when they have made a mistake and will look to avoid repeating it.

Explore what happened with them by asking what "we can learn" from the outcome (mistake) or asking "what could we do differently next time?" Avoid being judgmental or accusing.

If you are big enough to allow mistakes to be noticed but not reprimanded, you will be giving the other person a huge opportunity to grow, a spiritual gift, if you like.

Remember that fear of making mistakes cripples progress and the best place to start learning to handle other people's mistakes is to learn to handle our own. Forgiving yourself, especially if you are driven or a perfectionist, can be quite a challenge.

> Ask yourself:
> What do I need to risk?
> What is the worst thing that can happen if I get it wrong?

Motivation

When we do something we are so motivated by that it takes no apparent effort, we lose track of time and become present-moment-focused. When we are absorbed in whatever we are doing, motivation is almost a redundant idea; there is no motivation required, because in this state, things just get along by themselves. To motivate other people in this way, find a way of meeting their agenda as well as your own: that way motivation becomes self-motivation.

When someone is doing what is right for them, they are effortlessly motivated.

Motivation by being valued, praised and rewarded—financially or with affection—is fine and goes a long way, but the most powerful means of motivating is when someone finds interest and delight in the actual doing of the task itself. The very doing is the reward. This is far more direct than rewarding someone after the event: when the act of doing brings them joy, absorption or pleasure, their motivation comes from an infinite source because they are connected with a state of "being."

Ask yourself:

✦ What things in life motivate you so naturally it is no effort whatsoever to do them? What is special about the things that motivate you compared to the things you are not interested in?

✦ If you want to motivate someone, do you know what motivates them naturally? What is in it for them?

✦ In what areas of activity do they come alive? What kind of things are they doing when they are most self-motivated: creating, being technical, solving problems, interacting with people etc.?

✦ What would have to change for them to feel more motivated in areas of their lives where it is currently an effort? What else could they gain from those activities?

✦ How can you match what you want from them with what they want for themselves?

✦ Do you ever enter that state of being totally absorbed in something in the present moment? What things can get you into that state? What is it about those activities that make you do that?

✦ Can you find any of those qualities in things you do that you are not so interested in?

Nurturing Talent

By motivating others and helping them to find their true potential, you give them a very valuable gift, and you receive gifts from the situation for yourself too. Motivating people to expand themselves is a two-way street: as they expand into their talents, you share that expansion with them. Remember that nurturing your own talents and abilities, so you become as great as you can be, you inspire others to expand by following your example.

Things to do:
1. Practice delegating without emotion. Detach yourself from the response you receive. You never know what the response to your request will be until you have communicated it.
2. Practice making requests in different ways, until you find the key to each particular person.
3. Find ways to match your agenda with the other person's: that way, motivation becomes a joint effort and 1+1=3. Wow!
4. Look for ways to motivate and enable people in your relationships to become more of who they really are. Show the way by being motivated toward growing in yourself.

We have explored some ways to work with others to create and share the path to success. We have seen how the power of asking brilliant questions, motivating and delegating builds strength into your communications and relationships. Now it is time to learn about expressing our own personal power in Secret Eleven.

SECRET ELEVEN
Express Your Personal Power

Stallions can be creatures with great presence and personal power. They are loud and proud, they attract the eye, they are larger than life and exude incredible self confidence. So it was with one young stallion I had. When he was around, everybody knew about it. Which was fine if all you wanted to do was to stand back and admire him from a distance, but I actually wanted to ride this horse and work with him. The tricky thing was that much of the time he was so carried away with his own bluster, personal power, flush of testosterone and desire for the mares that it seemed that he didn't even know I was there.

One time I took this stallion to an old master horseman for some help with training him as a riding horse, but as I led him into the arena, before I even mounted him, he was prancing, neighing and pulling me about on the end of the rope as though I were invisible: no way was he ready for me to climb on his back and ride him.

And so this master, who rarely moved from his chair where he sat all day wrapped in coats, scarves, woolly hat, sheepskin gloves and covered in layers of blankets to keep himself warm, creakily rose from his chair, slowly and stiffly walking over to where I was hopping about, trying to hold on to this prancing white beast on the end of the rope.

The old master took the horse from me and began to walk. He walked no more than half a dozen steps and abruptly stopped. The master had apparently done nothing more than lead the stallion a few yards and stop, but by the time he had done this, the stallion had gone quiet, shrunk about thirty percent in height and was giving his full attention to the master: if a horse could salute, this horse was saluting. To see this was humbling, impressive and mystifying. After five minutes or so of the master walking with the now quiet stallion, he handed him back to me . . . and guess what? Of course, the stallion started acting up again!

So the question was this: what was different about the master? Since I couldn't see much difference in what he and I had done with the horse, the answer had to be his personal power. The horse felt it and so did everyone else in the room. The man displayed no false confidence, brashness or arrogance; rather, he showed a kind of personal power that is so sure, so inspiring, so self-reliant and attractive, that it didn't need to *try* to prove itself, even to half a ton of wayward male horse. In essence, it was as though he knew he could totally trust himself and the horse, so that his "knowing" manifested itself in his very "being," in the way he walked and stopped, and then walked and stopped.

To learn that lesson was about the hardest thing I ever had to learn around horses, and this horse had come into my life as my teacher. Did I learn it that day, that week or that year? No, and that lesson continues every day, whether I go near a horse or not, for what horses read of your personal power, and what people read too when the truth be told, is an internal quality that communicates outward from inside of us to others in a very subtle, and yet deeply moving way.

People whisperers express their personal power, presence, inner strength and are inspiring to others: along with those qualities they also show love, modesty and humility.

Personal Power

Much of this book is about personal power. By nurturing your personal power you improve your ability to communicate effectively, to make a difference, to be of value and to inspire others. Stepping into your personal power means learning to trust what you want comes to you, and that you are attractive when you are being who you really are. It means getting to know yourself and others, and being able to experience a life filled with more love and joy (and also to laugh at the whole thing!). This is why people whisperers do not shy away from stepping into the infinite personal power that is a part of each and every one of us.

What Is "Personal Power"?

True personal power is made up of many elements and is created by different people in different ways. There are, however, a number of factors that contribute to personal power.

If you have personal power, you have a sense of inner security that comes from your "centeredness"—you follow your own path and are true to yourself. As a result, others are touched by your model for life and are inspired to follow your example, thus you enable them to grow in their own personal power too.

Allow yourself to be brilliant and beautiful: it is your birthright.

Personal power has nothing to do with exercising command over other people: if anything, it is about having a high level of command over yourself. True personal power is "of the light," which means that there is no need to dominate others. It is totally secure in itself, seeking nothing from anyone else, which is why people find it so attractive.

Everyone has their own realm of personal power. It is an internal quality: you cannot look to anyone else to give you permission to claim it for yourself.

Inner Strength

It takes inner strength to live fully in society. Our modern, people-filled world can be a mentally and emotionally harsh place. Having inner strength means you can cope with the challenges of human life, follow your own path and still be true to yourself.

Inner strength means being who you really are and living as you wish, not allowing others to throw you about, to rock you emotionally or divert you from your course: you remain flexible, aware of your internal and external world, responsive, empathic, compassionate to others and responsible for your own actions.

Inner strength enables you to show your vulnerability and feel comfortable enough to appear weak, because you don't need to pretend or present a tough front to others. People are drawn to this kind of expression because they know it is totally honest. You are not attempting to fool any of the people any of the time: and that begins by not fooling yourself!

> However impeccably you conduct yourself, some people may react against a man or woman who has high levels of personal power and integrity, because it can challenge their own model of who they are.

Self-Reliance

Personal power is increased by being self-reliant, meaning being able to cope with life's challenges, supplying yourself with enough energy, resources, love and approval and not being "needy" of other people.

When you are self-reliant you can handle life because you trust yourself and the universe and know all things are temporary: nothing lasts forever, whether it is a good time, bad time, ecstatic time or totally and utterly impossible time. Whatever is happening and whatever other people are doing around you or to you, when you are self-reliant you keep your own peace, you listen and stay in touch with your body and remain centered, even amid chaos.

Being self-reliant means *you* decide how you feel: you respond instead of react and give love even in difficult circumstances. You are flexible and able to change what you do in order to respond to people or situations appropriately, bringing in fresh ideas and new ways of looking at things when needed.

Being self-reliant does not mean you don't consider other people or form meaningful bonds, quite the opposite. Because you do not need to feed off other people, you are more able to engage in healthy relationships, rather than seeking approval from others.

A self-reliant person does not need to take center stage, be the main focus of attention or do most of the talking: they are comfortable being who they are without public support or reinforcement of their worth.

To be self-reliant, avoid weakening yourself in relation to other people by doing any of the following:

- ✦ Attempting to impress
- ✦ Trying to justify yourself
- ✦ Asking for compliments or approval
- ✦ Giving someone too much attention that is not genuine
- ✦ Gossiping or making small talk to try to connect with someone
- ✦ Being falsely and overly concerned
- ✦ Trying to win favor
- ✦ Pretending to be interested in everything someone says

Personal Presence

Personal presence is a difficult thing to describe or rationalize: like other areas of personal power, it is can be made up of many different elements.

Presence is largely seen by other people as an outward quality, but it is really a reflection of internal qualities.

A person with true presence has a sense of self-worth and self-belief; they know their life purpose has value and that they are here to make a difference in the world. When they speak, it is because they have something they believe is important or worthwhile to say.

Let your light shine out into the world.

Someone with personal presence moves and uses their body in a centered and purposeful way. Their body and their energy communicate outward and touch people and at the same time, they hold their own space with confidence.

Someone with personal presence brings an energy with them you can almost touch: this comes from their sense of who they are and their focused awareness of their purpose.

It is not always appropriate in every situation or company to have your personal presence turned up to maximum. As you become aware of your presence, experiment with toning it up or down, depending on who you are with and what you want to achieve. Some people may find a high degree of personal presence a little too bright and may shy away, unless they are wearing their shades!

Being Inspiring

One noticeable quality of people who have stepped into their personal power is that they are inspiring. People who are inspiring have a vision they believe in, and that others can see and believe in too; they possess a quality that touches something in people, which enables others to release their own energy, creativity and action too.

An inspiring person sets an example of greatness and enthusiastic energy that helps people to see their own unrealized potential. When people see that projection of themselves in someone they admire, they are set free from their own limitations and spurred on to expand in their own way.

Ask yourself:

✦ Who inspires you and how do they do that?

✦ How do you inspire other people?

Someone who is inspiring gives the impression they are stretching themselves to achieve and be the best they can be; they excel at being who they are and communicate an enthusiasm which is almost contagious, making others want to be more like them in some way.

Modesty and Humility

The aspects of personal power discussed so far are potentially very powerful tools for people whisperers to have. That is why it is important to balance tools such as inner strength, self-reliance and personal presence with modesty and humility. Interestingly, there is great power in these qualities too, when they come from a place of integrity.

Being modest and humble can help to keep you grounded, especially when you have been exchanging energy at the high altitudes involved when you are in your personal power. Modesty and humility also prevent you from believing all your own press about your personal power and presence! Remember all of the qualities discussed in this secret must come from the right place; they are not born out of arrogance or a need for attention and the approval of others.

Things to do:

1. Don't be shy: dare to step into your personal power and be as magnificent as you can be. Remember that all people are equals underneath, which means you have as much potential for personal power as anyone else on the planet. That is an exciting and scary thought!

2. Look at ways in which people around you, either at home or at work, may try to make you less self-reliant than you could be. Trust yourself to know that you can cope whatever happens.

3. Develop a sense of presence: check in with your internal energy levels and sense of purpose. Allow your light to shine out into the world.

4. Remain grounded: remember that you need to be able to walk with your feet on the earth while you're still alive. Let modesty and humility keep you grounded and powerful at the same time.

Attraction

We have seen how people whisperers have high levels of self-reliance and personal power; that means they do not rely on other people for approval in order to feel attractive or needed. They know if they feel comfortable within themselves they attract all they need into their lives.

What Does Being Attractive Mean?

Being attractive means people want to share your time and company. It can mean more clients want to do business with you, friends want to walk that extra mile for you, people are drawn to you with a loving feeling or people want to rip your clothes off and make mad passionate love to you . . . Think about the possibilities that are opened up as more and more people find you attractive in a variety of different ways.

Physical looks

It is easy to assume that being attractive is primarily a matter of physical appearance and looks, but it isn't (thankfully!). Being attractive involves far more than just the way you look.

When we first see someone, there are a number of elements of attraction involved aside from a person's appearance. In addition to the way someone "looks," their body and its surrounding energy continually project that person's thoughts, emotions and intentions out into the world. And, although we may not consciously notice what the person's true self is projecting in this way, the signals they send out reach our unconscious and make them more or less attractive to us, regardless of physical beauty.

Ask yourself:

✦ What makes one person attractive to you and another person not attractive to you?

✦ What is it about some people that seems to make everyone find them attractive?

✦ And other people practically no one seems to find attractive?

✦ And more pressingly—how can we make ourselves more attractive to everybody?!

The illusion of physical looks

What you see when you look in the mirror is not what everyone else sees: what you see is your own interpretation of how you look. When we look at someone else, we often make automatic assessments, comparisons and judgments, however inaccurate, about what kind of person they are and therefore how attractive that person is to us. For example:

1. He's got long hair, he must be a lazy hippy.
2. She's wearing scruffy clothes, she must be a drop-out.
3. He's got a shaved head, he must be a hooligan.
4. She's wearing a nun's habit, she must be very devout and pious.

(See below for the truth!)

1. He is a famous actor who has grown his hair for a part in a lavish production of *Macbeth* for the Royal Shakespeare Theatre Company in England.
2. She is the chief executive of a major corporation on her way to help out at a local homeless charity, as she does every Saturday morning.
3. He has been receiving chemotherapy.
4. She is a call girl on her way home after seeing a gentleman with a taste for a particular habit!

Can we make other people find us more attractive?

We cannot make other people find us attractive any more than we can make them like a particular food. If you rely on other people to decide whether you are attractive or not, you make yourself a "victim" of their opinions. What you can do is change the way you view yourself, which often has the effect of changing how other people view you.

Before trying to change yourself or saying you *should* be different to how you are, take an honest look at how you are now. .

> Ask yourself:
> ✦ How much do you need to be "liked"?
> ✦ Can you feel happy with your own company?
> ✦ What messages does your body convey to others? What does the way you stand, sit and walk say about you? What does the speed and the way you move say about you?
> ✦ How do you feel inside about yourself?
> ✦ What thoughts and emotions drive you through life?
> ✦ What feelings do you wear on your face? What feelings do you attempt to hide from your face?
> ✦ What kind of "energy" surrounds you? What atmosphere do you bring with you when you enter a room or situation?
> ✦ What qualities do you already have that are attractive?
> ✦ How much do you rely on other people's opinions in order to feel attractive?
> ✦ What does the way you dress, your hair and makeup say or hide about you?
> ✦ Who are the most attractive people in your life? What makes these people attractive?
> ✦ Do you see any of those qualities in yourself? What could you do to increase these qualities in yourself?

Inner Self-Confidence

Probably the most universally attractive quality is inner self-confidence, but this doesn't mean you have to become egotistical or think you are better than anyone else.

Inner self-confident people are comfortable in their own skin: they have an inner peace and are accepting of themselves and others, which gives them a stillness that is attractive. By way of contrast, outwardly self-confident people rely on approval from other people or external events in order to feel good about themselves: consequently their self-confidence is a front. They are all huff and puff: "Aren't I marvelous?" or "See how the ground loves me to walk on it." This front is normally an attempt to hide their insecurity and it can make them uncomfortable company to be with.

Attraction that comes from your inner self is more reliable,
as it comes from an infinite source.

If you don't have inner self-confidence, how do you find it? As you follow the secrets contained within this book, answering the questions and following the "Things to do," you will be getting to know your true self and becoming more comfortable about your place in the world: this alone is the best nourishment to feed your inner peace and self-confidence. The more at peace you are within yourself, the more people, cats, dogs, horses, good fortune, opportunities and everything else the universe has to offer will be attracted to you.

You can't please all the people all the time!

We have been exploring how to become more attractive to more people, but we may not be successful with everyone. Well, tough, there's nothing we can do to control the people who are missing out on our delightful presence in their lives! Let them live with it; let them go, while we happily get on with being our true selves and enjoying our own lives.

> Take back your own power by deciding for yourself that you are attractive, whatever others may think.

Things to do:

1. Start noticing how special you are: look at all the things you can do that you normally take for granted. Something that seems relatively small and insignificant to you, like cooking lasagna or solving a crossword, may be a huge achievement in someone else's eyes.

2. Smile a lot and dress for you.

3. Take steps to build more inner self-confidence: remember self-confidence comes from being kind to yourself and nurturing a sense of inner peace within. Look at the section in Secret Two, "Eavesdropping in on your thoughts," and see what inner people whispering you do that makes you feel more or less attractive.

4. Shift your focus away from simply how you look on the outside: everyone looks the same on the inside anyway (roughly speaking)!

5. Drop expectations of other people and drop the need for others to approve of you.

Trust

There are many benefits to nurturing your personal power: one of those benefits is the increased ability to trust in whatever life has to offer. People whisperers know the value of trusting: trusting themselves, trusting comrades and loved ones, trusting professionals, trusting outcomes and trusting the processes of life.

Every time you get in an airplane you trust the pilot and every time you go to the doctors you trust them. Every time you eat in a restaurant you trust the chef, every time you drive a car you trust the other drivers, and every time you fall completely in love you trust your lover with your heart. Our whole lives are built on trust and yet when we are required to consciously trust we often find it hard.

This does not mean that people whisperers never expect to be let down; rather, they accept that people change, that nothing in life is for certain and all things are fluid, including trust.

HAVE YOU EVER TRUSTED SOMEONE AND BEEN LET DOWN?

If you have never trusted someone and been let down you are quite a rarity, as most of us have surely had this experience. This is one of life's fundamental lessons and one which gives us a choice: we can close down and shrink away from trusting people in the future, or we can use the experience to open further to life.

How can you ever know for sure someone can be really trusted? You can't: you just have to trust them! If you absolutely knew someone could be trusted, perhaps it wouldn't be "trust," it would be a certainty. "Trust" has an element of uncertainty about it: there is the possibility, however remote it may be, that trust may be broken.

> Trust has an element of uncertainty about it: that is what makes trust such a valuable and precious commodity—because it is possible to break it.

It is fair to say that trust can take a long time to build up and only a moment to destroy. But by refusing to trust anyone else in the future, you are stuck in a place where you continue to be hurt by the moment in the past when you were let down. If you spend your life believing you cannot trust, you are likely to create a life in which your trust is repeatedly broken.

Ask yourself:

✦ Who can you really trust? Can you really trust your friends, the government, employer, employees, business partner, kids, husband, wife, your husband or wife with your best friend!

✦ Here's an interesting question . . . can you trust yourself? Can you trust yourself to be worthy of your dreams, to be faithful to your own values, to be yourself and do what is right for you, to not let yourself down when it matters, to stand up for yourself, your principles or your loved ones if the chips are down?

CAN OTHER PEOPLE TRUST YOU?

Hopefully your answer to the question above is "yes." However, there may be times in your life when, even though you are an essentially trustworthy person, being true to yourself means you do something that runs contrary to another person's trust in you. This is because your beliefs or values may change during your lifetime, which means where once you could be "trusted" to be or do a certain thing, when your beliefs change you can no longer be "trusted" for how you were previously.

TRUSTING THE RIGHT PEOPLE

Here are some simple steps to take to help you to know how to trust the right people:

✦ Check with your inner self: how do you feel about this person? What are your emotions telling you about them?

✦ Use your intuition: what are your hunches telling you?

✦ Listen to your body: do you feel relaxed or uncomfortable?

TRUSTING "THE PROCESS"

Trusting the process means accepting the way people and situations are, and letting things develop and unfold as they are meant to without interfering. It can be a real challenge of trust for us to set things in motion and then let them happen, allowing them to run their course.

What we need comes to us, but we don't always know why people are doing what they're doing or why things are apparently more difficult than we think they should be. It is only when we look back (or see things from a higher perspective) that we can see the benefit or purpose of why processes happen in a particular way on life's journey.

Trusting the process means allowing events
to follow their course and turn out for the "best."

If you ever find yourself trying to steer people or events by pushing, cajoling and manipulating them to get a certain end result, or obsessively hoping things will turn out a certain way, you aren't trusting things will turn out for the best. By not trusting in the outcome, you interfere with the flow of the process and limit the space available for things to turn out in the most natural way.

If you trust people to play their part, yes, sometimes you may be let down or disappointed they didn't do things exactly how you wanted or expected them to do. But if you learn to trust the process, you can be sure the right outcomes will always find their way to you—often in ways that are different or better than those you expected.

TRUSTING THE UNIVERSE

Against all odds, we survive by living on the thin outer crust of a piece of mostly molten rock that spins constantly at about a thousand miles per hour, flying through space at heaven knows what speed, exposed to all kinds of physical threats, bugs, viruses, accidents, violence, meteorites, B movies, spam-mail and harsh environments—but we are still here. So how can we not trust the universe?

People who trust the universe don't just sit back and become couch potatoes: they are still active in the world, but they have a sense of being supported in it. They allow themselves to be in communication with the incredible, infinitely complex happening that is the universe and they flow with it.

> Think about it: if you trusted the universe to take care of you, to supply you with your survival needs, to bring you the people you needed, to keep you safe, to give you amazing experiences and learning opportunities, how much pressure would that take off you?

The next time you feel you have too much responsibility, you can't cope, things are running away with you, and you don't know how you're going to manage and you need more support, see if trusting the universe helps. Hand things over, trust in the power that created the Big Bang and put us here in the first place: remember that the power of the universe has infinite resources, which is even more than the United States has!

Things to do:

1. In what ways can you or can't you trust yourself? For example, can you trust yourself to be honest when it counts, to acknowledge other people's feelings or to do your personal best at all times? Most of all, can you be trusted to be true to yourself? Try it for a day or a week and see what happens.

2. How much can other people trust you? Are you reliable at work and dependable at home? Do you keep your word? When you appear trustworthy as far as other people are concerned, are you always being true to yourself?

3. Next time you are under pressure, trust that the universe will work things out? See if it makes you feel more comfortable, and whether any solutions appear that you hadn't thought of.

Holding the Intention
(and Softening Around the Resistance)

People whisperers know how to have intentions and trust those intentions to manifest for you. Your ability to "trust" is an expression of your personal power and another way to express that personal power is to "hold the intention and soften around the resistance." To do that requires complete trust.

People whisperers achieve this by creating a space, allowing people to play their part in the process and by not using the force of will to control events. It is simply a matter of asking for what they want and trusting the flow.

Anything is possible if you believe it

To create what you want, you firstly need to know what outcome you want. Many of us avoid choosing or naming what we would like to happen to us, for various reasons that are usually to do with our limiting beliefs. The truth is, if you believe something is possible and you deserve it, then it can happen for you.

Here is the reality:
anything is possible, and as a divine being, you deserve whatever
you wish for—whoever told you otherwise?

Pushing and *Trying* Too Hard

Once we know what our goal or outcome is, we humans normally start pushing to take control and make it happen. We think this is the way to overcome any resistance, whether that resistance comes from within ourselves (very common) or from another person or the universe. But what we perceive as resistance is not resistance at all: it is feedback, which means we need to ask ourselves what it is telling us.

You may need to invest energy, work and focus into what you want, but trying too hard with anything or anyone is uneconomical and ineffective, because it creates resistance.

Someone or something else can only offer resistance to you if you give them something to push against. If you soften, they no longer have anything to resist.

If you find yourself becoming involved in this proactive *trying* process and pushing through resistance, pause, take a breath, and step back. Soften in your body and mind about the whole thing. Let the tension drop from it and allow it to be. If you soften around other people they will have an unconscious sense of relief: you appear more attractive to them and they have the space to give you more of what you want. If you soften around the universe, amazing things start to come up for you; people will think you are plain lucky and life will expand beyond anything you imagined possible.

Softening around other people

If someone isn't doing what you want them to do, taking a longer time or going a different route to the one you want, avoid pushing them, getting impatient or interfering with them. The chances are they are going the right way for them at the right speed for them. This doesn't mean you won't achieve your final desired outcome; in fact you have more chance of achieving it if you soften around the resistance coming from other people and allow your intention to manifest itself for you regardless.

If you fight with someone to reach the outcome you want, you are investing your energy in the fight, not in the intention. If you achieve your intention by fighting, the outcome will not have the same easy quality that it would if you held the intention and softened around it.

It is worth remembering that the more something or someone means to you, the more challenging it can be to soften around the resistance.

Softening is not weakness

Of course you can disagree with someone over a principle, idea or behavior, but if you do it without a negative emotional charge, it will not give them anything to push against: it would be like they push against thin air.

Softening around resistance has nothing to do with "giving up" your goals, but it does mean giving up wasting energy and getting in the way. You have to be quite "in touch" with yourself and vigilant to avoid indulging in the typical human habits of pushing, trying or fighting to make something you want come about. This is not the same as giving up! Quite the opposite: because you are holding your intention and softening, your energy is quietly powerful and the universe or other people have plenty of space in which to deliver your intention to you.

> Often your intentions will come in ways you have not expected when you use this tool, often much better and much easier ... People may call you "lucky" ... hmmm, who knows?

Things to do:
1. Notice what you have been doing when things happen really easily for you. More than that, notice how you are being when things happen really easily for you.
2. Notice things that you obsess about, that you can't let go of and can't stop thinking about over and over. How ineffective is this and how much energy does it cost you?
3. Notice what your body is doing when resistance is present: see if you can let the resistance out of your body, by relaxing your shoulders, back or wherever else you habitually hold the resistance in you.

4. Drop the need to press or control others: remind yourself that none of this will matter to you in a hundred years' time.

When you communicate using your personal power, you express your birthright as a human being, which is even greater than you might imagine. In the final secret, we will discover how as human "beings" we are connected with one another and with the infinite magnificence of the universe itself.

SECRET TWELVE
Ask the Universe

It was a couple of weeks before Christmas and a friend persuaded me to have my palm read by a famous palm reader called Daniel Moon, who was based along fashionable Kings Road in London. One thing Daniel Moon said to me as he looked at my palm didn't make sense at the time: "The beginning of next year you will be doing very little, you could almost say you'll sit around in bed reading a book." One week into the new year and I came crashing off a horse and broke my wrist. At that time I made my living as a pianist in London, so working was not going to be an option and I told my music agent I would not be playing for a few weeks. (As it turned out, that event resulted in me changing the direction of my life completely, so all these years later my agent is still waiting for me to go back to work!)

So during January I found myself sitting in bed, just as Mr. Moon had predicted, reading a classic book on horsemanship by the great master Alois Podhajsky about the timeless tradition of how they train the riders and horses, the dancing white Lipizzaner stallions, at the Spanish Riding School in Vienna. One of Podhajsky's comments that stood out to me is that you cannot be a real horseman until you have started (broken in) and trained a horse fully yourself. At that time, as an amateur horse rider, that seemed like a phenomenally ambitious task for me to think of undertaking. Nevertheless, I wanted to become a "horseman"; I was desperately keen and set the intention that one day I would find a young horse to start and fully train.

A year or so later, my arm was fully healed and things had moved on. I was now living in the wilds of Exmoor working with horses, so I began looking for a quiet young filly (female horse) to start and train, as I thought this would be the most sensible choice for a first-timer like me to work with. What I had not figured on was that, because I had been poring over the pages of photos and tales of the dancing white stallions when I set my intention, the universe had been listening and was going to respond by giving me what I had unconsciously envisioned. Rather than a nice easy filly as my first horse to start and train, the universe was going to give me what I had really dreamed of and asked for: a full-blooded Lipizzaner stallion to break in and train.

I traveled throughout England looking for the right filly without much success, then one damp, gray winter's day, while looking at some horses for sale in the hills of deepest darkest West Wales, we saw a white stallion tied up in the shadows at the back of a cattle shed, his eyes gleaming, his coat shimmering and his presence being felt even through the near darkness. We asked the owners about him and they said he had only been used for stud duties on the mares and he was not for sale. Two months later they agreed to sell him and he arrived at our home, snorting, prancing, rearing and straining on the rope, his powerful muscles rippling, testosterone oozing from every pore as he announced his arrival and let every mare in the neighborhood know that he was here and ready for them. I remember thinking: "Oh my, what have I asked for!? Is this the first horse I am to start, to break in and to train: is this to be my greatest teacher, 900 pounds of breeding Lipizzaner stallion? What have I asked the universe for!?"

People whisperers are aware of what they communicate, not only to themselves and other people but also to the universe; and they understand that every communication is heard and responded to in some way by the universe.

Even when we don't intend to, we ask the universe for things. We even "accidentally" ask the universe for things we wouldn't want in a million years. When it seems fate is slinging a dreadful hand at us, it can be difficult to accept that we may actually have asked—intentionally or not—for whatever is happening in our lives. Never have truer words been said than those in the old adage, "be careful what you ask for: you might get it!" Because people whisperers are aware of this phenomenon, they are conscious of the kind of life and relationships they create in each moment through the messages they send out into the world.

There is a more positive side to the coin: if we are responsible for asking for the experiences and relationships we experience in our lives, it means we are in the driving seat. All we need to do is communicate—"whisper"—in such a way that we create the life we want to live. Wow! Anything is possible.

How to Ask for What You Want in a Way That Works

✦ Ask in a clear way and the universe will instantly start to set things in motion to answer your call, whether you are aware of it or not.

✦ Become aware of how you communicate with yourself, other people and the universe through your thoughts, words, emotions and actions. Start to see how these things are creating where you are now.

✦ Ask for what you want in a quiet and unattached way.

✦ Put your request out there, then stay out of the way and allow it to be answered. Resist the temptation to hassle and chafe about it. Once you have sent the message, let go. You wouldn't post a letter and keep hold of a piece of thread attached to it as it makes its way through the mail system, would you? If you did, it would never get to its destination. If you keep a hold on the things you ask, they will not be responded to because they will never really "get there."

✦ Recognize when your request is being answered, even in small ways. Sometimes the universe will communicate back to you by giving you a small sample of what you asked for, as if it is asking "Is this what you mean?" Show appreciation for any sign of your wish being fulfilled, even if in small ways, and the universe will understand what you want and give you more of the same.

Remember that everything in life is a stepping stone, another step along the way: there is no actual end, just more doorways to go through and more new territory to explore.

✦ Sometimes the universe hears our desire and gives us something different to what we expect. This is because our real self communicates a deeper underlying value or a need—different to what we thought we wanted. The universe gives us something to fulfill the underlying value or need, not our surface desire. E.g. we may ask to be slimmer and look more attractive. We don't get slimmer but shortly afterwards we meet a wonderful new lover. What the universe heard was the underlying message that we wanted love: the slimming was just our limited way of thinking we might improve our chances of attracting some love interest, but the universe heard the real request and knew the dieting was unnecessary.

Think about what underlying values you want to fulfill when you ask the universe and allow it to bring an answer for your highest good. You will not be disappointed.

✦ Phrase things in the positive and avoid using words like "don't," "can't" and "not"—e.g. "what I don't want is to be lonely in old age," or "I just can't ever see me finding my true love, my true soul mate" or "I am not going to find it easy to get another worthwhile job." The difficulty with this is that the universe will hear what you say and do its best to prove you right: so you are pretty likely to end up lonely in old age, not find your true love and not get a worthwhile job.

✦ Drop limiting beliefs. This means letting go of the thoughts you have about what is not possible for you in life. Those thoughts hold you back. How do you really know what is possible and what isn't?

✦ Notice how you communicate to the universe—through what you say, think or do—to bring you what you want. And notice how you communicate to the universe to bring you what you don't want. Remember the saying "Ask and ye shall receive." Yikes!

✦ The universe will bring you the right people you need. When these people arrive, all you have to do is recognize them and use your people whispering skills to integrate them into your life in a way that works for them and you.

✦ There's no need to SHOUT! You can whisper almost at the volume level of utter silence and the universe will hear you, provided the request you communicate is clear and congruent. Often the quietest, whispered requests are the ones most responded to.

Recognize the underlying "value" that you seek from a particular wish. Higher values—based on loving or generous acts—are more easily manifested.

Things to do:
1. Think of everything that has ever happened to you and all that is happening to you as though you had asked for it all. (OK, you may have been mad, but that's not up for discussion here!)
2. If you have asked for everything that has happened to you, even the tough bits, ask yourself what you may have wanted each

event to teach you. What did you potentially stand to benefit from it? If you can do this, you will be in a far more powerful and responsible place as a result.

3. Look at some of the people around you and see how they "ask" for what happens to them.

4. Experiment with "whispering" a wish or thought incredibly clearly and quietly, then let go of it. See what happens.

5. Practice "asking" for the relationships and life you want by doing more of what works and less of what doesn't. This may sound ridiculously obvious, but because of our attachments, patterns, habits and beliefs, this can be a bizarrely difficult thing to actually do!

6. Experiment with thinking thoughts to the universe that request the life, relationships and experiences that you would really like: be bold and ambitious. To reiterate, ANYTHING IS POSSIBLE!

Choosing Your Life's Companions

Life is sometimes a challenging, unpredictable and complex adventure, with many unexpected twists and turns. Each and every one of us is making our own journey and living our own life adventure. No one else can walk your path for you, regardless of how much you might wish them to, but what they can do is accompany you through life as companions, guides, allies and friends, making the journey more fun, exciting, full and fulfilling.

If you accept the idea that everything in your life is something you have chosen or asked for in some way, then that includes the people you share it with.

People whisperers are skillful at attracting and choosing good companions to accompany them on life's journey. They know the value of being with people who bring positive qualities to their life and lovingly nurture those relationships.

Our ability to select the right people as companions for the journey has a huge effect on the quality and experience of everything we do. The right companions can make the good times ecstatic and the tough times manageable.

Ask yourself:

✦ As you make your way through life, who would you like to have to accompany you?

✦ What kind of qualities do the people need to have to best help and support you in living your most loving, successful and ultimately fulfilling life?

✦ People need people, that's how we're made . . . what kind of people do you need?

With six billion people out there in the world, choosing friends and companions from among them can be some task! In a sense, everyone in your life has a role to play in your life's journey. These roles are very varied: partners, close family, work colleagues, friends, teachers, spiritual guides, lovers, rivals—the list is endless.

Fate, the universe, chance, luck or whatever you want to call it, will bring many people into your life. Some come to teach you; some to support you; some to stretch you; some bearing gifts; some to create magnificent experiences with you; some to challenge you; some to love you for who you are, and some—it may seem—to do nothing much at all!

It is up to you to decide who to keep in your life and who to pass by. You decide how to integrate people into your life and whether to create something worthwhile with them, or whether to squander the opportunities and special gifts that different people bring to you.

206 + SECRETS OF THE PEOPLE WHISPERER

Problem-Solvers or Problem-Makers

Wouldn't it be nice if other people could solve our problems for us? But unfortunately, no one else can, no matter how much we may like them to (although people sometimes appear to create our problems very effectively for us, don't they?).

Even if the people close to you can't give you the answers, they can help you to find them. Likewise, they cannot walk the path for you, but they can help you along the way.

The trouble is we sometimes invite companions along who seem to make the path through life even harder to walk, but it may be that the challenge of walking with these "difficult" people strengthens us for our own good.

Suggestion:

Think of every person who is significant in your life right now . . .

+ Are they currently helping or hindering you on your journey?
+ Are they making it easier or harder for you to live your life to its full glory?
+ If they are hindering you or making life harder, look for the gifts, the ways you may benefit from what they bring: we invite people into our lives because they bring potential gifts for us, whether they appear to or not.

On a scale of 1 to 10 (where "1" is making life impossibly difficult, "5" is they are neither adding nor taking away from life, and "10" is bringing incredible value to your life), give some of your current chosen companions a score. In what ways could you view each of them differently in order to score them more highly?

Positive Qualities—Positive Thoughts— Positive Language

The qualities you look for in your companions will depend to some extent on your own nature and the kind of relationships and experiences you want to create, but there are some general qualities which may be helpful if you find them in people you meet. What if you could build a fellowship of life travelers around you with some of the following qualities?

Loving	Trustworthy
Courageous	Talented
Kind	Understanding
Wise	Fun
Encouraging	Flexible
Good listeners	Willing
Helpful	Centered
Patient	Inspirational

Where would you score yourself (on a scale of 1 to 10) on the above qualities? In order to attract people with these qualities into your personal fellowship, it will help if you develop more of the qualities yourself.

Remember, you are traveling your journey with these people as your companions, but you will also be traveling their journey as their companions. The more "desirable" qualities you possess, the more worthwhile partnerships, associates and journeys you will be invited to join.

Light attracts light, positive people attract positive experiences: be around people who attract light and attract light yourself.

Things to do:

1. Think of your life as a journey and the people in your life as a fellowship of companion travelers. See how each of the companions you have chosen brings certain gifts, benefits and learning for you on your journey.

2. Enjoy the companionship of these other souls who have joined you. Feel a sense of connection and gratitude that they are willing to be a part of your story (but not your drama!).

3. Look at the roles you play in other people's fellowships and how you accompany them on their journeys.

4. Have a clear idea of the kind of people you want as companions and stay open to allowing them into your life: you will be amazed at who turns up for you. There is a saying: "When the pupil is ready the teacher appears." This could equally be applied to any vacancy you have in your fellowship: when you are ready to receive a certain person, they will appear, as a partner, business contact, teacher, valuable ally, enemy, competitor, great friend or soul mate ... the possibilities are endless.

5. See if you can catch yourself taking everything too seriously: remember, you, your life and the people in it may simply be acting out roles in a movie. Reality could be something altogether different to how we think it is!

Planning Chance Encounters!

During a lunch break on a workshop I was facilitating, a friend—who is a brilliant head of training and development in a multinational corporation—asked me an amusing and seemingly paradoxical question, "So, Perry, how do you plan a chance encounter?" In essence this question sounded like a contradiction in terms. But, in reality, much of what creates luck, possibilities and success can be put down to exactly that . . . planning chance encounters! The sort of chance encounter we are talking about could involve a life partner, business contact, helpful friend or someone you need but possibly thought you might never find.

People whisperers believe there are ways to increase good luck and to improve the chances of successfully bringing the right people into your life. To allow this to happen, they always seem to be in the right place at the right time and are willing to recognize moments of serendipity.

Creating chance encounters

Bumping into the right people will help you to live the life you want, so here are some questions to get you thinking about how to create chance encounters:

✦ What social and business circles do you move in?

✦ How do you encounter the right people? How do you know they are the right people? What do you do with them when you meet them?

✦ What invitations do you receive? What invitations do you create? What invitations do you give? What invitations do you turn down?

✦ What limiting beliefs do you have about your ability to meet people or to mix in different circles?

✦ Have you tried asking the universe for the person you want to appear in your life without worrying about how they will come? What might happen if you let go of limitations based on what you think is possible and allow the right person to come to you?

✦ How much are you pushing and trying, as opposed to asking for what you want and "allowing" it to come to you?

✦ What could you do differently in your life to open up new channels and allow new people to come in?

✦ Are you being too specific about the people you think you want?

Meeting the right people

How do you define who the right people are? In a sense, you could say everyone who comes into your life is the right person: it is what you choose to do or to make with the opportunity and person that will give you the belief about whether they are "right" or "wrong."

Whatever and whoever is in your life at this moment is right for this moment. You are always free to choose again, to reach out, and to move forward or sideways to create more chance encounters and bring new people in. It is what you make of those encounters that matters in the end.

How to nurture chance encounters

✦ Be in the right state when you meet someone; be your true self.

✦ Let go of any judgments or preconceived ideas.

✦ Be patient, give people time and hold the space.

✦ Be interested in other people for who they are, not for what they can do for you.

✦ Let them talk, ask interested questions, give them space to bring what they want to bring to your life.

✦ See what you could offer to them: it needs to be a two-way exchange.

✦ Speak their language.

✦ Avoid playing games.

✦ Trust.

✦ Take your time.

✦ If you need to, choose a good moment to ask for what you want in clear, direct language.

MARGRIT AND MY STORY

My first book was a specialist title about horse riding. When it was first published I did various appearances and shows to promote it at equestrian venues. One day some friends with a horse business asked me to share their stand at a small localized "equine fair" some distance from my home. Although I was reluctant to go—not least because I did not think that the sales on the stand would justify the cost—I agreed to do it, thinking, "Well, you never know who I might meet." I went along to the two-day equine fair with those words ringing around in my head. On the last day I left our stand to take a look around the others. One stand was for a regional newspaper which published a regular equestrian page, so I stopped to talk to the editor. She said she would like to run a couple of features about me—one about my horse book and one about my work coaching executives in leadership and communication—which I thought was rather exciting.

But that was only the beginning of a day of chance encounters, because the editor then turned and introduced me to a lady standing behind her, who had a pile of books laid out on the table. This lady was Margrit Coates, who is widely known for her healing work with animals and for her books, *Hands-on Healing for Pets* and *Healing for Horses,* copies of which she was signing. I spent some time talking to Margrit and we exchanged contact details and swapped books.

As a result of that meeting with Margrit, an incredible chain of life-changing events and opportunities have unfolded and continue to unfold for me. Margrit and I formed a partnership and produced and recorded an album of healing music that became the record company's best-seller of the year. I now continue to produce music both with Margrit and as a solo artist for the same record company: this is more significant if you appreciate that I had previously spent over ten years attempting to get a recording contract and not succeeded. Margrit also introduced me to new clients for my corporate coaching business; but more exciting than all of that, she was instrumental in this book—*Secrets of the People Whisperer*—being published. Wow! How "lucky" was all that?

All because of one "planned chance encounter" in an unlikely setting. Going to the fair with the idea that "you never know who you might meet" had opened the way for the universe to send someone my way who was to have a huge influence and benefit on the following years of my life and career.

The story of meeting Margrit Coates gives a very obvious example of planning a chance encounter. Of course, chance encounters usually happen in more subtle ways and they aren't normally preempted with a phrase such as "You never know who you might meet," but it shows just what can happen when we hold intentions and are open to possibilities. Of course, some people would say my meeting was down to pure luck and if that is what they want to call it, well, I guess they are right. My question in response to that would be "Well, what can I do to allow more of that kind of 'luck' to happen?"

Coincidences and Synchronicity

Think about the following:

✦ Do you see life as a bunch of accidents happening to you, one after another: some good, some bad and some indifferent?

✦ Do you think people fall into your life like the chance tumble of a dice?

✦ Do you think the chaos theory is chaotic?

✦ Do you notice how many coincidences are happening in your life?

✦ Have you ever met someone and then said "What a small world"?

✦ Have you noticed how, once you start to recognize coincidences, they seem to keep happening more and more?

Things to do:

1. Go somewhere different to your usual haunts: put yourself about a bit! If your social life has a routine to it, change the routine for a week or two and see what happens.

2. Do something you have dreamed of doing, and not got around to so far. Make sure it is something that will bring you into contact with people you don't know.

3. Ask your unconscious, or the universe, or whatever power you believe in, for what you want to happen, and then forget about it.

4. Start noticing coincidences: the more you notice them and acknowledge their happening, the more they will start to work for you.

5. Always be your true self; be the best, most natural person you can be.

Soul Connections

On one level, we are all ONE. We are all connected. We are all a part of the same universe. There is no separation. This can be a challenging idea to accept, because society and everyone within it acts with such self-interest that the idea of separation has become normal to us. The idea of separation develops in us as we grow up from babyhood. As babies we are not aware of any separation; we experience ourselves as a part of the same whole as our environment and everyone in it.

People whisperers believe we are all connected and are all part of one creation; they always have a sense of connectedness and approach all people with understanding and empathy, because they see themselves in every other person.

We are all connected on a physical level too; we just don't have a constant awareness of it. For example, if a giant meteorite hit the earth, who would die? Probably all of us! We are all connected by our existence on the same planet: we share the same home, circulate the same resources, such as water, and breathe the same air as one another. When a nuclear accident happens thousands of miles away, we too are affected. Even our genes go back to the same few sources. We are all part of this vast creation; we are all part of humankind: behind all the behavior, we are all one.

✦ If you had a sense that we are all part of the same "oneness," how might that alter your dealings with each and every person in your life?

Dissolving the Gap

To fully experience our soul connections, we have to see our self as the other person and the other person as us. That means we sense no gap or space between us and any other person; whereas we normally feel there is an "us" and a "them."

214 + SECRETS OF THE PEOPLE WHISPERER

One definition of love means identifying others as part of yourself, and yourself as part of them. Imagine looking at a sunset: instead of "you" looking at the sunset, you become a part of the moment, part of the picture of the sunset. Rather than just being the onlooker, you are in the picture and an integral part of the scene.

Being able to experience the "connection" between us has huge potential when it comes to our encounters with other people. If you can sense the connection without experiencing a gap between yourself and others, you will find it easier to drop judgment, to understand the other person more deeply, and to feel full compassion and empathy for them. Experiencing the connection means you won't be inclined to erect barriers or create difficulties that hinder your interaction with the other people. You will find people being inexplicably drawn toward you.

Connecting with love

The word "love" carries with it all sorts of interpretations and connotations, but what we are talking about here is not just the love that makes us romantic, cutesy or nicey-nice. The love we are talking about is beyond all of the human expressions such as words (which is why I'm struggling here!). It is powerful and is a supreme state of awareness: in it, we are totally open but also safe.

> By bridging the gap or divide between us,
> in a sense we actually become love.

This level of soul connection can exist between you and anyone, should you choose to recognize it. Sometimes words are not enough: those are the times when you need to communicate on a soul level. If you are in a conversation and find you share no common ground whatsoever with the other person, you can still connect with them on a soul level by consciously dissolving the gap between you. As you can imagine, this opens up huge possibilities in areas where conversation is difficult, in all kinds of situations and relationships. We can all do this—you can do it, anyone can do it. However, be aware that attempting to use a soul connection to influence someone else intentionally for your own gain does not really work: the universal law of love will not enable you to control others in this way.

Recognizing Soul Mates

It is a strange phenomenon that out of the vast number of people with whom we have contact throughout our lives, there are usually a few with whom we experience a special connection—sometimes even on first meeting them. In truth we have a soul connection with everybody, but it is easier for us to recognize ourselves mirrored in some people than others.

For example, have you ever met someone and hit it off with that person straight away: you feel like you already know them—you have so much to say and seem to have so much in common? What is that about? Sometimes, even before you really talk to someone new there may be a sense of "recognition" between you: they seem familiar, even though you haven't met them before. Some people explain this experience by saying it is about knowing each other in past lives. Well, I can't honestly remember living before so I can't comment about reincarnation, but whatever is actually happening, encountering a soul mate is a profound and wonderful experience.

Why do soul mates come into your life? As the sense of recognition is very real, let's accept that the reasons for their coming are significant and very real. Enjoy the opportunity to spend time with people who come into your life in significant ways. By allowing things to unfold gradually between you, you will discover what gifts you have for them and what gifts or messages they have for you.

Distance Communication

Have you ever noticed how it is sometimes possible to communicate with people—without using technology such as the phone or Internet—despite there being a huge distance between you? Many of us in modern society find it difficult to believe in this level of communication: after all, how could we possibly hear someone communicating with us over huge distances? You don't believe it either? What about radio: do you believe in that?

There are many records of animals and people, often belonging to older tribes such as those of the African Bushmen, who appear to be able to communicate over great distances with those with whom they have close relationships. As with so many of our innate skills and instincts, in the Western world we have lost touch to a large degree with these parts of ourselves. We can liken losing these skills to the way that a muscle will waste and the neural pathways to that muscle go to sleep when they are not used for any extended period. As with a muscle or neural pathway, it is not impossible to reawaken these skills, but it does require regular use and practice. A quote from the *I Ching*, a Chinese oracle from three thousand years ago, says:

> ". . . Whenever a feeling is voiced with truth and frankness, whenever a deed is the clear expression of sentiment, a mysterious and far-reaching influence is exerted. At first it acts on those who are inwardly receptive. But the circle grows larger and larger. The root of all influence lies in one's own inner being: given true and vigorous expression in word and deed, its effect is great . . ."

With openness and a soul connection, you may find you can communicate with someone not necessarily in words, but with an aligned sense of being. You may discover after the event that someone with whom you have a soul connection was talking about the same unlikely subject as you were on the same day but miles away. Or you go to pick up the phone to dial someone but the phone rings and it is the person you were going to call who has called you instead.

Although we are almost totally unaware on a mental level, which is where most of our attention in life is placed, there can be much communication happening on a soul level, and since distance is irrelevant at the soul level, this can happen with someone anywhere else in the world.

Things to do:

1. Become aware of the fabulous gift of soul connection you have with certain people. See these people as huge blessings in your life.

2. Let yourself be open to the idea that you are connected to absolutely everyone. Actually you could take it beyond the people you see, and feel that connection with the whole of your surroundings. Just because other people don't recognize the same level of connection, or they even act obnoxiously toward you, doesn't mean you are not connected on a deeper level. Sometimes people may act even more obnoxiously toward you because your soul connection with them makes it "safe" for them to do so.

3. Start to notice when people at a distance from you appear to be thinking along the same lines.

Conclusion

The ways of exploring people whispering are infinite. In working our way through the twelve secrets, we have looked at everything from awareness of our own physical, mental and spiritual communication through to how we interact with the universe and others at soul level. Here are a few more final thoughts—golden nuggets—for you to reflect and expand upon:

- ✦ Keep communication clear and simple.
- ✦ Try less and allow life to flow.
- ✦ Be aware of the fear of being vulnerable: remember that a newborn baby is about as vulnerable as a human can possibly be, but it still gets taken care of.
- ✦ Timing is so important: if you carefully time your communication with someone, their response will be much more favorable than if your timing was inappropriate. You have to develop patience and sensitivity to how people feel and where they are "at," in order to have great timing.
- ✦ Flexibility is a key skill to have around people. Life is in a constant state of flux; nothing stays the same, including people. To be the best you can be and allow others to be the best they can be, don't assume that doing what worked before will work the same next time: it may not. Move with the flow and be flexible at all times. Doing A may result in B on one occasion: and another time may result in X!
- ✦ Gossip . . . does not do anyone any favors!

✦ Age: ask any adult and I think you will find that most people, especially the elderly, feel about seventeen to twenty-one years old. That is an interesting thing to bear in mind when talking to someone of seventy-five!

✦ This is your life: it is not about anyone else or what they would do. Listen to people's opinions, by all means, but at the end of the day, choose what you feel and know to be right for you.

✦ Keep moving forward. If you try to go backward in life or ponder too long on what happened before, such as how someone hurt you or let you down, you will miss what is happening now.

✦ Be encouraging to yourself and anyone else that is around. Encouragement brings a positive boost of energy to people.

✦ Laugh more than you would normally!

✦ Remember that life is short: if possible, make your peace with the people around you, without compromising yourself in the process.

✦ In any situation where you are stuck or don't know what to do, come up with at least three options and then choose one. You may be in a situation with someone where you don't think you have any options, and externally that may be true, but you always have options about how you communicate with yourself or how you feel.

So, who is the people whisperer? In reality, we all have a people whisperer inside us: an adept, sensitive and skillful communicator who is often hidden behind a mask of conditioning and automatic responses born out of fear, social expectations and limiting beliefs, or buried under the weight of coping with everyday life.

The wonderful thing is, when you begin to remove all that is not you, it allows the people whisperer within to surface and communicate with yourself, other people and your environment with a newfound level of joy, engagement and success.

As you practice the methods of people whispering and integrate them more and more into your communications, relationships and life, you will begin to discover another secret: that opening yourself to the art of people whispering—the gift of communicating—is an ever-expanding process. There are endless possibilities to be uncovered along the way.

May you discover the people whisperer within you and may the gift of communication enhance your own life and the lives of all those beings with whom you share your world.

The People Whisperer's Glossary

Appropriate: This is a very useful word when talking to someone about a difficult area or behavior. By saying you don't feel something is "appropriate," you are making a clear statement that it is not suitable behavior, without sounding like you are accusing or blaming the other person. It is difficult for someone to argue with a statement like "I don't feel it is appropriate for me."

Awareness, self-awareness and other-awareness: This means noticing what is going on. If you notice what goes on inside you—emotionally, mentally, and physically—then you are self-aware. If you notice those things in others, you are "other-aware." And if you notice those things in the universe you are in danger of being referred to as a guru or crackpot, depending on the viewpoint taken by others!

Boundary: This is a line drawn in the sand, a way of stating to others what is acceptable to you and what is not. It is not a confrontational stance, but a clear message.

Buttons (as in "pressing"): In this context, the word "buttons" has nothing to do with undoing your shirt, it means saying or doing a certain thing to get a reaction from another person (normally an emotional one). People close to you may be especially good at pressing your buttons and making you react this way.

Choices: Like making a selection of what you want from a menu, choices are how you decide what you want life to dish out to you—a gourmet feast of incredible, loving, fun experiences or a plateful of indigestible difficulties. This is also about how you decide to respond to the dishes you are served and how you feel about them.

Compassion: This is a sense of empathy and love toward someone at a heart level, born from the feeling that, underneath, we are all the same.

Controlling: This means attempting to impose your will on someone else to direct their behavior and limit the choices which are their natural right. It is a form of behavior that comes from not trusting in the flow of life and being run by our fears and insecurities.

Empathy: Being empathic means understanding, accepting and identifying with someone else's feelings or situation. It is not the same as being sympathetic, which is more akin to feeling sorry for someone and is not particularly empowering for them.

Energy: Everything is made of energy. Eastern religions have been telling us this for thousands of years and scientists have recently caught up and agreed! Everything is filled with energy too: a stone, thin air, your thoughts, love, your body—everything contains energy. Energy can appear inert or "apparently" inactive, but it is still present in huge amounts. Think about the amount of energy released by splitting the atom in an atomic bomb; now think how much energy you have contained within your body, which is made up of countless trillions of atoms. What could you do if you released that energy and used it for good?

Flow: This describes the natural state of everything; the way it is all meant to happen, freely, easily and without resistance.

Hope: This is often seen as a positive word, e.g. "Where there's life there's hope." But "hope" really does leave plenty of room for things not to turn out right—it is often about handing over power to someone or something else.

Intention: An intention is something you intend to do. It is more positive than "want to do," "would like to do" or "hope to do." Intention gives a clear message that you are committed to the arrival of a particular outcome. For example "I intend to give up smoking tomorrow" is more powerful than "I want to try to give up smoking tomorrow."

Love: This is the most powerful force in existence; it is the material that binds everything in the universe together. Love is inside, outside and around everything, although much of the time we don't notice it, partly because we are also made of it, but more because we are so wrapped up in thinking and doing. Every communication is an exchange of love on some level or another. When we are aware of love, the feelings of ecstasy, bliss and awe it brings are . . . ecstatic, blissful and awesome!

No: With only two letters, "no" is one of the biggest words in our vocabulary. It can be a hard word to hear from someone; it can also be a very hard word to say to someone.

Purpose: This is what you are really here for, what you are meant to do with your life and where you can best place your intentions and energy. Once you find your true purpose, all kinds of inner resources and energy are made available to you.

Pushing: This is when someone tries to use their determination or weight of personality to force an outcome or result. Pushing often creates counter-resistance, i.e. pushing back. It is not a very energy-efficient way of having relationships or achieving goals.

Should(n't): This is a very "parent-like" word, which carries an implication that if you don't do what you "should" do, you will be bad or wrong. It is a word that implies a moral judgment and says that your words, actions or events in life are expected to be a certain way, which they often aren't! For example, I should be good at doing this by now; you should be earning more money; the tenants upstairs shouldn't be so noisy when they're having sex on Sunday mornings!

Soul: This is your life energy, the essence of who you really are. It is infinite, untouchable, eternal and divine.

Space: This is the empty, free territory between everything. It is becoming quite rare on earth, both physically and mentally. We tend to fill every available space with thought, word, action or "stuff." Having more space, even for a moment, allows new insight and fresh possibilities to be created. Although we perceive there to be emptiness between events and objects, it is actually filled with divine energy or love, as is everything and everywhere. That means that space is also a form of love, if you can figure that one out.

Other Ulysses Press Mind/Body Titles

1001 Little Health Miracles
Esme Floyd, $12.95

A treasure trove of friendly health tips that offer shortcuts to feeling good, looking great and living healthy.

A Chorus of Wisdom
Edited by Sorah Dubitsky   Foreword by Stephen and Ondrea Levine, $14.95

Essays from over 25 visionary thinkers that offer insight and revelation in a manner that is sure to bring positive change.

Courage After Fire: Coping Strategies for Returning Soldiers and Their Families
Keith Armstrong, L.C.S.W., Dr. Paula Domenici and Dr. Suzanne Best, $14.95

Provides a comprehensive guide to dealing with the all-too-common repercussions of combat duty, including posttraumatic stress symptoms, anxiety, depression and substance abuse.

Yoga for 50+: Modified Poses & Techniques for a Safe Practice
Richard Rosen, $14.95

Focusing on the needs of the beginning student 50 years and older, this book details the basic principles of yoga and teaches yoga poses through the use of step-by-step photos, clearly written instructions and helpful hints from the author.

How Meditation Heals: A Scientific Explanation
Eric Harrison, $12.95

In straightforward, practical terms, *How Meditation Heals* reveals how and why meditation improves the natural functioning of the human body.

One Soul, Many Lives: First-hand Stories of Reincarnation and the Striking Evidence of Past Lives
Roy Stemman, $12.95

This remarkable collection of true stories brings together an impressive body of physical evidence and fascinating accounts of reincarnation.

Stop Living Your Job, Start Living Your Life: 85 Simple Strategies to Achieve Work/Life Balance
Andrea Molloy, $12.95

A successful personal life coach shows how to identify priorities, make meaningful decisions and take specific actions.

Unlocking the Heart Chakra: Heal Your Relationships with Love
Dr. Brenda Davies, $14.95

Applying the techniques of the chakra system, this book examines the central relationships in our lives and offers a plan for understanding them.

To order these books call 800-377-2542 or 510-601-8301, fax 510-601-8307, e-mail ulysses@ulyssespress.com, or write to Ulysses Press, P.O. Box 3440, Berkeley, CA 94703. All retail orders are shipped free of charge. California residents must include sales tax. Allow two to three weeks for delivery.

About the Author

Perry Wood is a ground-breaking coach, workshop leader, horseman and author. He originally studied music at London's Guildhall School of Music, and worked as a professional musician until 1990, when he gave up his music career and moved to Exmoor to work full-time on his horsemanship.

Perry successfully transferred the communication skills he developed from horse whispering into people whispering. Now a recognized authority on communication, he regularly appears in the national media, including network TV, and is asked to contribute to leading magazines and newspapers.

Senior executives in major corporations benefit from Perry's coaching, teaching and inspirational workshops on communication and leadership skills. He also works with individuals and couples on their life and relationship issues.

Perry is the author of a number of equestrian books, including the widely acclaimed *Real Riding*, and continues to lead horsemanship and riding clinics worldwide. He lives in southwest England with his partner, two dogs and seven horses.